IMAGES
of America

FOLEY'S

Twerp ·······
Where our two careers
in this crazy classroom began!
What great memories ······

" Toots "

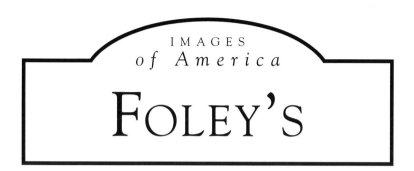

IMAGES
of America

FOLEY'S

Lasker M. Meyer

ARCADIA
PUBLISHING

Copyright © 2011 by Lasker M. Meyer
ISBN 978-0-7385-7928-3

Published by Arcadia Publishing
Charleston, South Carolina

Printed in the United States of America

Library of Congress Control Number: 2010922852

For all general information, please contact Arcadia Publishing:
Telephone 843-853-2070
Fax 843-853-0044
E-mail sales@arcadiapublishing.com
For customer service and orders:
Toll-Free 1-888-313-2665

Visit us on the Internet at www.arcadiapublishing.com

*To all the Foley's associates and executives over the years
whose hard work made Foley's one of the largest and most
profitable stores in the United States. Their contribution to
the cities in which Foley's stores were located is missed by the
many civic organizations they supported and served.*

CONTENTS

ACKNOWLEDGMENTS

Unbeknownst to most of the management group at Foley's, Robert "Bob" Dundas, senior vice president for publicity and community affairs, kept letters, interoffice memos, photographs, store documents, and copies of the store newsletter in boxes for 50 years. When the management of Federated Department Stores, of which Foley's was a part, bought the Macy's group and decided to change the name of Federated Department Stores and its stores to Macy's, it discontinued local management, moved control of Foley's to Atlanta, and changed the name of Foley's to Macy's. At that time, Ed Smith, who remained in charge of Foley's community affairs office, donated Dundas's archives to the Houston History Archives, which is a collaborative venture between the Center for Public History and the University of Houston Libraries. Dr. Teresa Tomkins-Walsh, the center's historian and project archivist, kindly gave me access to the 50 boxes, even though they had not yet been formally processed. I owe her and the staff at the university's archives repository thanks for their help and support on this book.

I also owe thanks to my daughter, Susan Meyer Sellinger, who accompanied me on each trip to the university and provided great help in going through the many boxes of uncaptioned papers for several days and hours. She also provided needed help in grouping the photographs and articles in proper order on the computer so they could be properly provided to the publisher.

Unless otherwise noted, with few exceptions, all photographs are in possession of the Special Collections Department of University Libraries at the University of Houston and were owned by Foley's or, in some instances, by the author and his daughter, Susan Meyer Sellinger. Two of the images were part of the Bob Bailey Studio Photographic Archives at the Briscoe Center for American History at the University of Texas. Finally, thank you to the Sloane Gallery collection (www.sloanegallery.com).

INTRODUCTION

The real story of Foley's cannot be told in pictures alone. The secret of its success was twofold; its merchandising philosophy and organization melded to make a culture different from many of its peers. From the very beginning, under the original two Foley brothers, Foley's merchandising philosophy combined one-stop shopping with competitive pricing and anticipated many of the merchandise trends that did not dominate the industry until decades later. Although many department stores discontinued certain departments in the face of discount store competition, Foley's kept them as major supporters of the strategy that said low margin departments with high volume, while not necessarily profitable on their own, absorbed a large amount of indirect store expenses, which ultimately allowed the higher margin departments to be more profitable. It believed in structuring its merchandise assortments to serve all but the highest and lowest 10 percent of the population in its market areas. At one time, it had departments such as outdoor furniture, lawn mowers and fertilizer, photographic supplies, a pet shop (with monkeys), stamps and coins, piece goods, major appliances and television sets, and a drug department complete with a pharmacy. Few, if any, of these departments are found in department stores today.

Three merchandising innovations stand out in Foley's history. First was the inclusion of Italian-style men's clothing. Second was the development of the very first calculator department in a department store. Under the guidance of Joe Sternberg, Divisional Merchandise Manager, Foley's started carrying early calculators from manufacturers such as Commodore and Texas Instruments. They were an instant success as Houston had a large base of engineers because of the oil industry. Hewlett Packard, which made very specialized calculators carried only in technical stores and college book stores, at first refused to sell to a department store, but after seeing the success of the department agreed to sell Foley's as its first department store. The department was a million-dollar success.

The third innovation was the development of a men's fragrance and cosmetic department. Up until that time, major women's cosmetic companies only sold men's products to the women's department, which typically gave them little space and attention. Foley's management recognized that by standing alone in the men's area it would appeal to more customers and would get more attention by having its own buyer. Almost every cosmetic company in the country resisted, but Foley's management held firm in its belief. In a few short years, Foley's had the largest men's fragrance department in the country and was the major customer of every supplier.

Other key decisions led to Foley's success. It, along with Humble Oil (now Exxon Mobil) was deeply involved from its very beginning in every aspect of the Houston community, and Foley's associates at all levels were found in civic, cultural, and charitable organizations in every city in which it had stores. At one time during the Great Depression when banks were closed and customers couldn't cash checks, Foley's, along with Henke & Pillot (a major grocer in Houston at the time), cashed checks for its customers and issued them Foley's backed scrip that was accepted as cash all over the city. As the company began adding branches in Houston and other Texas cities, two other decisions played major roles in the company's growth. First of all, each branch, while not necessarily the same size as another, was treated as a first-class citizen with similar assortment only limited by the size of the store. This meant that the quality of merchandise and the price ranges carried were similar in 85 percent of the cases. The second decision was that Foley's would not go into a remote city unless the size of the store, or the need for multiple stores, would allow Foley's to dominate retailing that city. This contrasted with other department stores that were satisfied to have one store in a city and be the number two or three volume retailer in that city. These two decisions played a major role in having Foley's stores be among the highest sales per square foot of any store in Federated Department Stores. Of course, the fact that Houston and Texas both were growing dramatically helped achieve those results.

Finally, another major factor in Foley's culture, was the belief of developing the management of the organization from within, rather than going out and hiring from other stores. Every senior level executive either started on the training squad or at a very low management level in the store. Due to this philosophy and the fact that Houston became a very desirable city in which to live, Foley's lost very few of its executives to other stores unless it was a promotion within Federated Department Stores. This was due primarily to a management choice to push decision-making to the lowest possible level, giving executives the authority commensurate with their responsibility. Foley's buyers and divisional executives went into the markets with the authority to make decisions that often required higher-level management approval in other stores.

CHIEF EXECUTIVE OFFICERS

1900–1917	Pat and James Foley
1917–1945	George S. Cohen
1945–1963	Max Levine
1964–1978	Milton Berman
1979–1982	Stewart Orton
1982–1987	Lasker Meyer
1988–1990	John Utsey

One

THE BEGINNING

In 1896, when Houston was a small town compared to Galveston, the W.L. Foley Dry Goods Co. opened in a small building in what is now Market Square near the landing where the Allen brothers first decided to build a city. W.L. Foley operated his store until his death in 1925, and his children managed the business until 1948.

More importantly, Foley was the "rich uncle" who, in 1900, lent $2,000 to his nephews, Pat and James Foley, to open their own store, a 20-foot-by-70-foot building at 507 Main Street. Stocked with calico, linen, lace, pins, needles, and men's furnishings, the store recorded opening-day sales at $113.12. The total number of sales was 138, and the largest individual sale was $8.75. George H. Hermann, who gave the park bearing his name to the city, and those others prominent in Houston affairs were listed as early customers of the Foley brothers.

In 1900, the city of Houston (which was named for Gen. Sam Houston, the hero of the battle of San Jacinto that was fought nearby, and the first president of the Republic of Texas) had a population of 44,000, which had taken 64 years to attain. The 1850 census gave it a population of 1,396; in 1870 the population was 9,382, and in 1890 it was 27,000. Beginning in 1900, a series of events took place that greatly accelerated the growth of Houston with considerable benefit to Foley Bros. and other Houston stores.

The first and most spectacular of these events was the disaster that overtook the neighboring and rival port city of Galveston on September 8 and 9, 1900. At that time, Galveston had no seawall. The city itself was at or below sea level. A tropical hurricane hit the city, bringing in its wake a devastating tidal wave. The dead, many of whom were swept out to sea, numbered between 5,000 and 8,000, and property damage was estimated at $50 million—a huge sum at the time. The author's father, who was five years old then, told stories of the family drilling holes in the floor of the house to allow the water to rise without sweeping the house away, and of the children being tied to doors so they would float in case the house was destroyed. After the storm, many Galveston residents moved to Houston.

The second event occurred the following winter, when Capt. Anthony F. Lucas began to drill for oil on Spindletop Hill, near Beaumont, less than 80 miles east of Houston. Four previous attempts had ended in failure, but at a depth of 1,160 feet on a January day in 1901, tremendous gas pressure blew several tons of pipe from the hole with a deafening roar and spouted oil nearly 200 feet over the top of the derrick. This gusher marked the start of serious oil activity in Texas. Oil production for the state jumped from 835,039 barrels in 1900 to 4,3393,658 in 1901, and in 1902 the Spindletop Field alone produced 17,401,000 barrels. The development of other gulf fields followed, and many oil companies found it convenient to make Houston their headquarters.

In 1902, the first big step was taken toward making Houston a deepwater port, despite the fact that it was 50 miles from the Gulf of Mexico. On June 13, 1902, a bill was signed appropriating $1 million for the Houston ship channel from Galveston as far as the suburb of Harrisburg. This improvement eventually made Houston the second American port in deep-sea tonnage and third to New York and Philadelphia in total tonnage. Foley Bros. grew at the same time. The original 10 employees were joined by Frank J. Matzinger, who previously had been employed by the brothers' uncle. He became a cashier and had an office on the mezzanine floor to which cash and sales slips were dispatched by an overhead basket system. Matzinger eventually became treasurer and assistant secretary of Foley Bros. and spent nearly 50 years there.

In 1905, the store acquired the property next door and added women's and children's ready-to-wear clothing and millinery. Three years later, in a second expansion to keep pace with the city, the store moved to a location in the 400 block on Main Street. In 1911, the capitalization of the store was $150,000.

By 1916, Foley Bros. ranked third in retail volume in Houston with $400,000 in sales. The original 10 employees had grown to 150, and the company had 750 active charge accounts and 23,000 square feet of space.

W.L. Foley's first store opened in 1876. Foley was called the "Dean of the Mercantile Industry in Houston." He established his store in 1876 at the 200 block of Travis. The building, which had been used as a Confederate armory during the Civil War, was given to Foley by his father-in-law, John Kennedy. The store sold French imports and ladies' piece goods and notions. Foley died in 1925, and his store was closed in 1950 by his daughter Blanche. She sold the Foley's name to Federated, who then dropped the "Bros." and kept Foley's as the official name.

A customer's car is parked in front of Foley Bros. at 507 Main Street. W.L. Foley lent nephews Pat and James Foley $2,000 to open this store, which recorded opening-day sales at $113.12. By 1916 Foley Bros. recorded $400,000 in sales.

A truck delivers merchandise to the 20-foot-by-70-foot building, which was stocked with calico, linen, lace, pins, needles, and men's furnishings. At the time, Houston had 44,000 residents.

This is the expanded store owned by Pat and James Foley at 400 Main Street. The store was moved to this site in 1908.

Two

1917–1945

In Galveston, Robert I. Cohen, the owner of the largest store in that island city, watched Houston grow at a rapid pace as his own city still recovered from devastating hurricanes in 1900 and 1906. He also had another problem to solve: his restless son, George S. Cohen, was anxious to spread his wings outside of Galveston. Both problems were solved when Robert decided to purchase Foley Brothers and put his son in charge in 1917. He was not completely confident of his son's ability to manage such a large investment, so he sent his office manager, Leopold L. Meyer, to keep an eye on the financial management of the business. Meyer, the son of a modest Galveston rag and scrap iron merchant, grew up in a large family consisting of eight brothers and one sister. The sister, Esther, married George Cohen and moved to Houston with him. Eventually, after World War I, six of the brothers ended up at Foley's, as did their father, Achille. Each brother managed a section of the business: Leopold (Finance), Leon (Men's, Piece Goods, and Home Furnishings), Hyman (Women's Accessories and Small Wares), Lasker (Children's, Lingerie, and Misses Sportswear), Arthur (Ready-to-Wear, Coats and Furs), and Marcus (Operations).

Foley Brothers took a leading role in Houston's World War I activities. Large advertising space was devoted to Liberty Bonds with captions like "Free Men buy bonds—slaves wear them." The store sold only bonds at certain hours and served as a depot for overseas packages. In May 1918, Foley Brothers employees made the largest Red Cross flag ever displayed in Texas and carried it in a parade that was 10 blocks long. Some $700 was tossed onto the flag in the course of the march. Thus began a history of civic involvement by the management and employees of Foley Bros. that lasted for nearly a century.

Even before the war ended, Cohen began to improve the store. Additional space on Prairie Street was leased in June 1918. At Christmas, a special shopping service for men, staffed by male salesmen, was inaugurated. The store became the representative for Vogue patterns, which were exclusive in Texas at that time. Sales totaling $500,000 in 1918 increased to $985,000 in 1919. The store did a sizable business in war surplus goods, even selling gas masks at 95¢ each. In the spring, the millinery department was expanded to absorb the entire third floor and became the largest in Houston. The store advertised more, varying its morning and evening newspaper copy, which was an innovation in Houston at the time. In 1920, a famous local newspaper columnist wrote, "However our confidence in Foley Brothers is so great that we are almost prepared to guaranty any ad they put out." Much of Foley's advertising in this period was written by Cohen himself. He used a number of slogans but emphasized, "You never pay more at Foley Bros." Foley Bros. developed a reputation as a store with large assortments and low prices that eventually was repeated in later years and ensured its reputation as the place for Houston consumers to shop for generations.

These efforts combined with Houston's prosperity to give the store a record volume in 1920. Though Dallas was still larger, the census takers that year counted 133,350 persons in Houston, an increase of 78 percent more than a decade earlier. Foley Bros. sales in February were 34 percent more than the same month in 1919. March and April were each up 53 percent. May was up 57 percent. At the end of that month, Cohen returned from a buying trip to New York, convinced that the postwar inflation had gone too far. He announced that he was joining John Wanamaker, the famous Philadelphia and New York merchant, in cutting retail prices. With the enthusiastic endorsement of the local Housewives League, he began to slash prices in July. Silk hose, bought at $33 a dozen were sold at $1.98 a pair. An Enrico Caruso concert and George Cohen's advertising of "the New Dollar" and its greater purchasing power were topics of Houston conversation in the fall of 1920. Foley's sales for the year totaled a record $1,500,000, and there was a small profit in spite of the price-cutting. Several local competitors had losses.

While a large part of the country suffered a severe drop in business in 1921, increasing oil prices kept Houston and Foley Bros. busy. "Depressed New York furnishes bargains to prosperous Houston through Foley Brothers," Cohen wrote in a widely reproduced advertisement announcing bargain purchases. At a meeting in a local newspaper office attended by Jesse Jones and other Houston leaders, Cohen, as spokesman for retailers, accurately predicted that Houston's diversified interests would enable the city to escape the Depression felt in other parts of the country.

The record $2,225,000 volume for 1921 gave Foley's valid claim as the largest retail business in Houston, and the store promptly expanded into larger space as well. In January 1922, Foley's paid $300,000 for 17,500 square feet of historic Main Street frontage adjoining the store. Gen. Sam Houston had originally purchased the property for $100 on December 1, 1838. The enlarged store was opened formally on June 24, 1922. In the following August, a shoe department was added. In December, a 15,000-square-foot Basement Store, the first true bargain basement in Houston was opened. To bring in customers, excursions in the form of free streetcar rides from anywhere in Houston were offered. Sales dropped back slightly to $2 million in 1922, due primarily to the reduced prices.

In the fall of 1923, Foley Brothers added a beauty salon. In August, the store was closed for an hour to permit employees to attend memorial services for Pres. William G. Harding in the Iris Theater. Some months later, employees attended a similar service for former Pres. Woodrow Wilson.

Capital stock of Foley Brothers was increased from $150,000 to $500,000 on February 2, 1924, with all shares remaining in the hands of the Cohen family and their immediate associates. In June, the store became the first in Houston to adopt the eight-hour day. Store hours were nine to five. Adoption of the eight-hour day was praised by the mayor of Houston, the Housewives League, the YWCA, the Brotherhood of Railway Trainmen, and other organizations.

Cohen was a leader in bringing the Better Business Bureau to Houston. Foley Brothers became a charter member. In 1924, Foley Bros. endorsed the 24-point "Truth in Advertising" campaign of the Associated Advertising Clubs of the World.

Foley Bros. opened a boys' clothing department in 1925. It was one of three authorized Boy Scouts of America outfitters in the Houston area and the only store authorized to sell official Girl Scouts clothing and equipment. As Foley Bros. had long sold phonographs, the addition of the new radio sets was a logical one.

Foley Bros., which had already expanded horizontally, now expanded vertically with the central portion increased to nine stories. The work required three years. When it was completed in 1927, Foley Bros. boasted 175,000 square feet of floor space, 1,000 employees, more than 30,000 charge accounts, sales at the rate of $5 million a year, and a payroll that supported one percent of the population of Houston. At some point in time, from then into the next century, it was hard to find a family that did not include someone who once worked for Foley Bros..

One of the features added to the store in the expansion was an auditorium known as Town Hall. This was made available for civic enterprises and as Houston then had no municipal auditorium, it was much in demand. The Rice Institute Alumni Association met in Town Hall, as did Texas Company's employees. The Houston Symphony rehearsed there. At Christmas time, Town Hall was used as the largest toy department in Houston. Throughout the rest of the year, it was used on Saturday mornings for talent shows. Movie and stage dancing star Ann Miller made her first appearance there as a child actress in one of the talent shows. The same shows also played at the expense of Foley Bros. in surrounding towns for the benefit of Parent Teacher Association and similar organizations. The jazz orchestra and chamber music ensemble of Foley Bros. employees also used the hall regularly. Another feature of the expansion was the eighth-floor restaurant, Spanish Town, which was available to smaller women's clubs and other civic groups as well as to store customers for special events. Sunken Garden, a restaurant with counters and tables, operated for a time in the basement and a cafeteria was provided for employees on the top floor.

A feature on the seventh floor that few saw was Cohen's private office, protected by his longtime secretary, Margaret Doyle. It was copied from a room he had admired in Florence, Italy, but all the materials were American and came from Houston if possible. The office had a feature rarely seen in any office of that time or since: a complete barber chair where he received a daily shave and occasional trim from one of the male barbers in the beauty salon.

The 1930 census gave Houston a 292,353 population, the largest of any city in Texas, and a gain of 111.4 percent over the 1920 figure. As soon as this was announced, Foley Bros. adopted the slogan "The largest store, in the largest city, in the largest state." A prominent picture of the store in 1936, the time of the Texas Centennial, shows the slogan painted on the side with the additional statement "Owned by Texans, Operated by Texans."

In the dark days of the 1933 bank holiday, the store's reputation for integrity was dramatically recognized. With foresight, Cohen withdrew enough cash to meet the payroll. With the banks closed, personal checks were no longer generally honored, but Foley Bros. was so well known that the store's checks were accepted. As a service to its customers, the store accepted checks from its customers and in exchange wrote checks for odd amounts and, along with similar scrip from Henke & Pillot, a 61-year-old grocery firm, this served as money for Houston.

Robert I. Cohen of Galveston, who was Cohen's father and one of the owners of the store, died in October 1934. Following his death, Foley Bros. was reorganized with the younger Cohen becoming president and his six brothers-in-law, the Meyer brothers, becoming directors as well as vice presidents. In 1934, the store expanded further with the purchase of 22,000 square feet of adjoining property. In an effort to encourage home improvements, Foley Bros. organized Foley Brother Finance Corporation in 1935 under a state charter for the purpose of making Federal Housing Administration Loans.

A procession of famous visitors kept Foley Bros. in the news during the late 1930s. Gloria Morgan Vanderbilt and her sister Thelma, also known as Lady Furness, came to the store to introduce Sonia Fashions. Irene Castle came to launch her hats. Coleen Moore, a famous former motion picture star, exhibited her fabulous dollhouse for the benefit of crippled children. Bridge experts held exhibitions and authors autographed their works. Since my father was one of the Meyer brothers and my uncle was George Cohen, I was exposed to retailing at an early age. One of my first memories is going to Foley's with my father, who worked in his office on Sundays when the store was closed. There was no one else in the store, and I used to commandeer one of the elevators and spent time racing up and down from the basement to the ninth floor. I was allowed to work small jobs in the store each summer. In my possession is a handwritten note from my uncle Leon Meyer sent to Ben Epstein, head of personnel, dated September 7, 1934, when I was eight years old. The letter states, "Lasker Meyer Jr. worked for me for two days and his services were extremely satisfactory and I can recommend him for any job in the store." Each summer, I got experience in a different area of the store, always working behind the scenes. One of the most boring positions was the summer spent in the accounting department filing customers' charge slips in long drawers that had a folder for each customer, so they could be charged at the end of the month. One of the most interesting jobs I had was the summer spent in the display department under the watchful eye of Eddie Rose, head of display. I don't remember what I did, but it must have been important! Finally, a few years later, uncle George allowed me and two of my closest friends, Meyer and Ralph Minchen, to open a model airplane department on the eighth floor, outside of Town Hall, that operated every Saturday. A club was started for the young customers and special silver wings were made that were given to each club member. Thus began my retail career.

As Houston continued to grow, reaching a population of 384,514 in 1940, the store became too crowded. Thought was given to possible construction of a new building in the growing business section farther to the south on Main Street. Cohen purchased 37,500 square feet of land on Travis Street and obtained an option to buy for $1,250,000 the First Presbyterian Church site of 31,250 square feet on Main Street. The outbreak of World War II prevented further action.

With the entry of the United States into the conflict, Foley Bros. channeled its advertising, much of its store space, and many of its personnel into the war effort. Full-page advertisements, sometimes partly in color, were give to the Red Cross, the USO, and other war activities. During certain busy hours, the store sold only War Bonds. Robert Dundas, the store's publicity director, served as vice chairman of the War Finance Committee, which attracted national attention by quickly selling enough bonds to build a new cruiser, *Houston*, to replace the one sunk fighting a Japanese fleet in the Sunda Strait. Thousands of overseas parcels were dispatched by Foley's, and the store also acted as a depot for the collection of musical instruments for the Armed Forces.

Foley Bros.' gross sales in 1943 were $5,222,292.10. They were $6,592,455.33 in 1944, and in 1945 they were $8,007.593.91.

In 1917, Robert I. Cohen, a Galveston merchant, purchased the store from the Foley brothers and made his son, George S. Cohen, president. Expansion came with the new management and by 1919 sales had reached $985,000.

George S. Cohen, chief executive officer from 1917 to 1945, was married to Esther Meyer. Her brothers all held management positions at Foley's.

An advertisement announces the change of ownership and the change of name to Foley Bros. Dry Goods Co.

Pictured are the eight Meyer brothers of Galveston and their sister Esther. George Cohen married Esther and after World War I, six of the eight brothers joined Foley's in various management positions. The brothers are, from left to right, Lasker (Children's and Intimate Apparel), Leopold (Finance and Office), Leon (Men's and Home Furnishings), Arthur (Ready-to-Wear and Furs), Morris (a lawyer), Marcell (a lumberman from Yoakum, Texas), Marcus (Operations), and Hyman (first floor departments.)

A move in 1922 to a three-story building next door gave the operation more space. A 15,00-square-foot Basement Store was added and Foley Bros. became the largest store in the city. In 1927, five more floors were added. The store then had 175,000 square feet of floor space and 30,000 charge customers.

This window display from the store at 400 Main Street promoted the notions department. Foley's has always been known for its elaborate displays.

Early-20th-century Foley Bros. had beautiful wooden fixtures such as this one in the men's department with a display showing a summer suit and straw hat.

This is a view of the first floor, looking back to front, with prices ranging from 7¢ to 50¢. For sale is body powder for 50¢, talcum powder for 15¢, and insect powder for 7¢ among a host of other items. Since the Houston air can be sweltering, ceiling fans were used to try to cool the sales floor.

Handkerchiefs used to be de rigueur for women as well as men. This photograph shows the extensive array of ladies' handkerchiefs. No retail department such as this exists in today's department stores.

In the early 1900s, many of the clothes worn were made at home, creating the need for stores to carry an extensive selection of sewing accessories.

Although fashion trends for men have come and gone, ties and dress shirts remain a wardrobe staple just as they were when this image was taken, although one might be hard-pressed to find a tie today for 98¢. Take note of the jaunty boater hats on the back display case.

This is another view of the men's section with caps and hats perfectly arranged in the display cases. At the end of the men's section, one can also see a mannequin wearing a woman's blouse and skirt from the period with the advertisement "Navy Wear for Travel Wear."

After the turn of the century, Americans were on the move, mostly by train and car. Foley Bros. had an extensive luggage department to serve its customers' needs and carried items as varied as small valises to trunks. At the left of the image are round hatboxes emblazoned with designs such as a flying bird or a tropical scene.

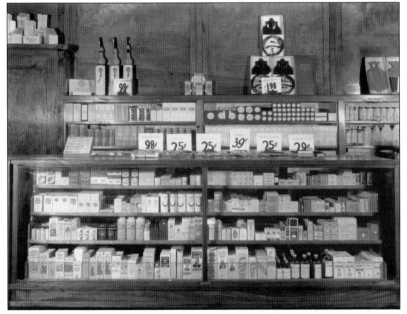

Foley's was a true department store in that it even carried items typically found in drugstores. This is the drug department where items such as combs, liniment, medicinal teas, hot water bottles, and castor oil were sold.

The ability to stay in touch with loved ones who lived far away was achieved through letters and notes, hence the need for decorative or elegant stationery to write on. And of course, stationery couldn't be used without a proper pen.

Ribbons were used for everything from clothing trim to hair bows; hence the need for bolt after bolt of ribbon.

A child's layette included the usual gowns and booties, but take special note of the cases filled with bonnets and hats. Also note the monochromatic scheme—hopefully, the child liked white.

Foley's Bros. was "the Christmas Store" and recommended that their customers "Shop Early for Christmas" and to please "carry their packages."

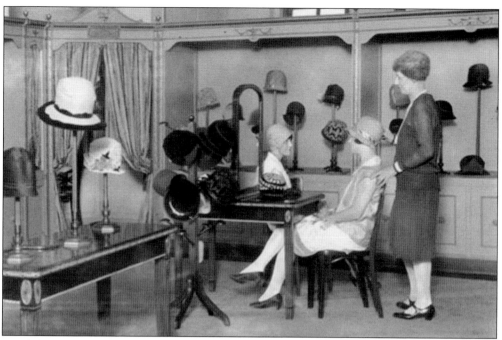

Until the 1960s, a lady's complete wardrobe included the perfect hat to complete her ensemble.

Each incoming or outgoing call had to be manually plugged into the proper connection by a switchboard operator. And, of course, there was no voicemail!

Ensuring that all Houstonians knew their Christmas theme, Foley's Bros. advertised their Toy Town, found on the eighth floor, on the outside of their building.

Doing double duty, Foley's also used its advertisement for men's Van Heusen shirts on the side of the building to promote war bonds, which were central to the home front efforts to support American involvement in World War II. As mentioned in the introduction, during certain busy hours, the store sold only war bonds.

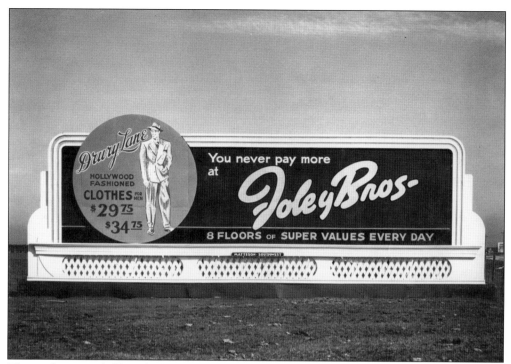

This mid-century billboard advertised "Hollywood Fashioned" clothes for men at the downtown store. Note that this advertisement also calls attention to the eight floors of selling space, as well as one of the company slogans, "You never pay more at Foley Bros."

Outside of Knapp Chevrolet sits a brand-new fleet of Foley's delivery trucks that the store used to deliver merchandise to its patrons.

These images look north (above) and south (below) down Houston's Main Street. Foley's was at 400 Main Street. Taken during the 1928 Democratic National Convention, these photographs show flags along the street that represent each of our 48 contiguous states. Al Smith was the Democratic nominee for president, and Herbert Hoover won the election. This was the first convention in the South since the Civil War. (Both images courtesy of the Sloane Gallery collection.)

Three

THE FEDERATED YEARS

While nobody knew it at the time, the future of Foley Bros. would be affected greatly by an Army order that in 1941 assigned young Lt. Ralph Lazarus of Columbus, Ohio, to Ellington Field, near Houston, where the US Army Air Forces conducted a navigation school. Lazarus was a member of the famous department store family and was the eldest son of Fred Lazarus Jr., president of Shillito's in Cincinnati and also president of the newly formed Federated Department Stores. Federated consisted of Abraham & Straus of Brooklyn, Bloomingdale's of New York City, Filene's of Boston, F&R Lazarus Company of Columbus, and Shillito's of Cincinnati.

Fred Lazarus Jr. came to Houston to visit his son, and having some hours to wait before the officer came off duty, toured the business district and inspected Foley Bros. with a professional eye. He was impressed with the bustle of the city, which by now was the largest city in the South. On later visits, he became enthusiastic about Houston as a logical city for Federated Department Stores expansion.

As a result of studies and surveys, Federated Department Stores management decided to aggressively pursue a location in Houston. The management met with George Cohen and offered to buy the store. They were turned down. Lazarus then told Cohen that if they would not sell Foley Bros. to Federated Department Stores, then Federated Department Stores would build a major competitive store near Foley Bros. in the downtown area. George Cohen felt the best decision was to sell. The Meyer brothers, most of whom were younger, did not want to sell. Since Cohen held the majority stock, however, the decision to sell was made after negotiations that lasted nearly four years. Of particular dispute was whether to include the property that had been optioned from the First Presbyterian Church on Main Street for $1,250,000. Leopold Meyer, in particular, was adamant that the piece of property not be included in the deal. After further negotiation with Federated Department Stores, George Cohen made the decision to include it. As a result of that decision, Leopold Meyer and George Cohen, who were brothers-in-law, did not speak for the balance of their lives. All of the Meyer brothers resigned shortly after the deal was consummated. The decision to include the Main Street property was not a good one. Federated Department Stores bought Foley Bros. for $3,599,310.87. Lazarus made the decision to sell the church property for $3,000,000 plus the $55,000 promised to the broker. Famed promoter William Zeckendorf came down from New York to offer Lazarus $2,750,000, which the broker urged him to take. "Look," Lazarus told the broker, "if you haven't sold it for $3,055,00 by the end of the month, the price is going to go up another $250,000." On the deadline, a Woolworth's agent called Lazarus and said, "Are you the Mr. Lazarus who put this outrageous price on that real estate in Houston?" "Yes," said Lazarus. "Well," said the agent, "I'm not going to pay it." "If you don't pay it today," said Lazarus, "it will cost you $250,000 more tomorrow." In the end, Woolworth's paid it. It became known as the "$10,000 a front foot deal." From that deal alone, Federated Department Stores recouped much of its initial cost of acquiring Foley Bros. Leopold Meyer was right.

Active direction of Foley's was entrusted by Federated Department Stores to Max Levine, who first served as vice president, director, and general manager. He became president on June 3, 1946. Levine was a 1925 graduate of Harvard Business School. He worked at Abraham & Straus, Federated Department Store's Brooklyn division. After several job changes, he joined the F&R Lazarus Company in Columbus, Ohio, as basement merchandise manager, remaining in that capacity until coming to Houston. Also sent to Houston was Maurice "Mogey" Lazarus, who became vice president of services and control. He had been the first floor merchandise manager at Shillito's after graduating from Harvard. At that time, the name was changed to Foley's.

Steps toward a large new building for Foley's were taken immediately. The property previously purchased was not large enough for the new store, so a site of 63,000 square feet on a city block bounded by Main and Travis Streets and Dallas and Lamar Avenues was purchased for $1,974,000. At that time, the new location was at the southern end of the business district. Foley's selected Kenneth Fransheim of Houston, who was famous for his work on the Gulf Building, as an architect. Raymond Lowey Associates of New York, the most famous store interior designer of the day, was selected for the interiors. Ground for the new store was broken on March 1, 1946. Mayor Otis Massey made this comment at the ground-breaking: "I think that any organization which assumes such an important share in community life becomes more than just a business—it becomes an institution of which all the citizens of the community can be proud. We Houstonians are proud of Foley Brothers. We will be proud of Foley Brothers' new building . . . but I think we will be even more proud of the things we cannot show to our visitors—the community spirit which makes Foley Brothers a vital part of our city's life." This comment, made in 1946, was to be the guideline for the part that Foley's management and its many employees played for the next four decades. There were few, if any, civic or charitable activities in the community in which Foley's didn't play a major role. This approach made Foley's "their store" to generations of Houstonians.

Foley's executives were involved in every aspect of civic life in Houston, often heading up organizations such as the United Way or the Fat Stock Show and Rodeo. Ray Miller, a longtime newsman who has chronicled Houston history wrote, "Foley's wasn't just a business, it was a way of doing business. It had character. The president of Foley's was somebody and had great civic responsibility." That devotion to Houston and its many facets of life also involved many of its "associates" who also spent many of their off hours in various Houston activities. In Foley's archives are hundreds of letters, some from ordinary citizens, some from the most famous names in Houston's past, some from major civic organizations like the symphony and the Fat Stock Show, and some from tiny PTAs from school districts in remote counties. A favorite letter, written on stationery from the *Houston Defender*, reads, "I am enclosing herewith a check for seven dollars and fifty (cents) for the balance due on the Frigidaire that I purchased from you some several months ago. I want to express my gratitude and appreciation of the unusual and almost incredible cooperation and kindness of the company in assisting me to liquidate this obligation. My business fell upon evil days shortly after I purchased the box, but you people were more than kind. I shall never forget it and will, where possible, buy from Foley Brothers." To publish every letter in the archives would require another book, but suffice it to say that every segment of the Houston community benefited from its largesse. It was that type of community involvement the made Foley's the unique institution it was.

The new six-story brick structure was windowless except for massive plate glass show windows. At the front were huge curved windows, flanked by large glass doors recessed from Main Street. These Main Street windows became linked to the memory of Houstonians, young and old, as the location of the famous automated holiday scenes, visited by thousands of people from Houston and elsewhere each Christmas. It became a family tradition to take the children to see the windows each year.

At the center of the building were escalators, a relatively new innovation and the delight of all, particularly of youngsters who enjoyed riding to the top and down again many times. Because of the large volume of traffic, the escalators were timed to operate at a faster speed. There was a soda grill in the basement, a tearoom on the third floor, and an eating place for men on the second floor. Facilities for employees included a large cafeteria on the sixth floor, lounges, recreation and game rooms, and a sundeck on the roof. There was a small hospital on the sixth floor. Hundreds of automobiles were accommodated in the parking garage built across Travis Street with a tunnel running under the street to the basement of the main store. The total cost of the store was $9,000,000.

When Foley's opened its new store at 1110 Main Street, it established the southern end of the retail business in downtown Houston. Although Sakowitz eventually built a marble emporium across the street from Foley's, no other store ventured south on Main Street.

When Foley's moved from its 510 Main Street location, it sold the store to Joske's of San Antonio. Joske's was comparable to Foley's, but Foley's management outsmarted them by putting in the agreement to sell that Joske's could only carry home furnishings and was not allowed to have any fashion clothing departments. This was a major error in strategy for Joske's, and prevented the store from being a factor in Houston retailing until it finally moved to a store in the newly developed Galleria many years later.

Retailing in Houston was composed of Foley's, Sakowitz, Battelstein's, the Smart Shop, Byrds, and Walter Pye. With the exception of Foley's, all were family-owned businesses. When the Meyer family left Foley's after it was sold to Federated Department Stores, they bought five suburban junior department stores called the White House Stores. Within a few years, the name was changed to Meyer Brothers. Although there were some single stores located in suburban areas, this was the first time that a group of stores carrying moderately priced, branded merchandise was located in the suburbs. They expanded to 10 stores including ones in Pasadena and Texas City. Shortly after, the Palais Royal group of stores also began opening in the neighborhoods of Houston. Ben Wolfman's The Fashion sold its downtown location to Neiman Marcus of Dallas, which opened its first store outside of Dallas in a downtown Houston location and eventually moved to anchor the Galleria.

Houston continued its postwar growth, and Foley's grew along with it. The original six floors were expanded to nine, and its sales and profit continued to increase.

In 1959, Meyer Bros. sold nine of its 10 stores, keeping only the Meyerland Shopping Center location (no relation). Although several of the original Meyer brothers continued to own and run the business, the author decided to leave after 13 years in various merchandising and store management positions. After several attempts to find comparable employment to the position and salary I held at Meyer Bros., I was interviewed at Foley's by Charles Luft, who was then in charge of merchandising, and was offered the position as buyer of the boy's 8–20, Boy Scouts, and Western Shop departments. At that time, blue jeans didn't enjoy the popularity they have today and the only department in the store carrying them was the Western Shop. Although the salary was below the amount I had been earning at Meyer Bros. and the position was at a lower level, I decided to join Foley's. There was some disagreement among Foley's key executives as to whether I should be hired; Les Dewald, head of personnel, felt the company shouldn't hire me because I would only stay a short while and move on to greener pastures. Credit should be given to Max Levine for agreeing to hire me, because my father and his brothers left Foley's on bad terms.

The first year that I was a buyer of the boy's 8–20 department, I had gone to the Rice Hotel, where many traveling salesmen showed their lines to buyers in those days. I had a disagreement with the salesman because I refused to write my order in his showroom. I preferred to write my orders after shopping all competitive lines, whereas the salesman wanted me to write it immediately under pressure from him. He insisted on my writing it, so I left the hotel and went back to my miniscule office at Foley's. Not long after, the door opened . . . and in walked Max Levine. In those days that was an unheard of experience. If management wanted to talk, the employee was summoned to management's office. I was sure Levine was there to fire me! He said, "I understand you had a disagreement with one of our important resources about writing an order." I said "yes" and explained my reasons. He said, "I just want you to know that I support whatever decision you make." Needless to say, my feelings about working for Foley's and its management were strengthened substantially. That was particularly important because, in less than a year, I was offered a higher management-level position and salary at Battelstein's and turned it down because I felt that, long-term, Foley's offered more opportunity.

On August 6, 1958, the big headline in the *Houston Press* was "Bomb Plot at Downtown Store Foiled! FBI Jails 2." Three young white males were arrested for planting a fake bomb in the downtown Foley store and asking for $50,000, or else they would plant a real one. The FBI moved quickly, identified the men, and found bomb supplies in their car. On that same day, the newspaper announced the opening of the new home furnishing floor on the seventh floor of Foley's. It was more than 64,000 square feet and had 32 model rooms. The Dow Jones that day was 513.88 and down as a result of the oil crisis caused by the threat to close the Suez Canal.

Shown here is Foley's in 1944. Although it was the largest store in Texas, Fred Lazarus, the head of Federated Department Stores, was not impressed. He felt it did not compare with the large Eastern stores. He was impressed with Houston and its future, however, and made an offer to buy Foley's. In 1945, the deal was completed.

A headline in the *Houston Chronicle* on May 22, 1945, announced the building of the new Foley's store and that Foley's would become part of Federated Department Stores.

This photograph shows the Foley's store under construction on a city block bounded by Main and Travis Streets and Dallas and Lamar Avenues. Ground was broken on March 1, 1946.

To develop interest in the new store, a Sidewalk Engineers Club was formed. The fence around the store had peepholes so interested people could watch the construction, and radio stations produced daily programs on the site, as seen here.

As the store nears completion, the sidewalk barrier is still in place. The six-story structure, built at a cost of $9,000,000, would later be expanded to nine floors.

The modern garage across the street was connected to the store by a tunnel under the street. It was designed so that a conveyor belt could bring the customer's packages to the garage by way of a conveyor belt from any floor in the store.

FOLEY'S

Tops in Texas

Each day brings it nearer completion . . . the $10,000,000 shopping center which will bring to Houston and Texas the most modern merchandising and service facilities in America today . . . a New and Greater Foley's . . . living up to Houston's tradition for being "Tops in Texas."

FOLEY'S

The Foley's public relations machine was hard at work, whetting the appetite of Houstonians by announcing the near-completion of what became a $10,000,000 store.

Mr. Fred's Dream Store

By RAY JOSEPHS

America's darnedest new department store has walls
without windows, delivers parcels to cars by gravity.
The jet-propelled methods of Fred Lazarus in Houston
have paid off—may profoundly affect American retailing.

NOBODY has ever quite figured out why a woman who goes into a department store to buy nothing more than a packet of bobby pins, often ends up purchasing two pairs of shoes, a toaster cover, three scatter rugs and a $1.98 slip. But a good many people, among them Fred Lazarus, Jr., have tried to find out. A short, energetic experimenter of sixty-five, Mr. Fred, or Mr. Junior, as he is known in the murderously competitive mayhem called retailing, has often done his researching in unconventional ways. He's listened behind the adjustment counter, swept floors, sold collars, and, reportedly, once had the corset-fitting room wired to catch the uncensored comments before determining if customers preferred slide fasteners to hooks on the two-way-stretch foundations.

This effort has not been without some success, considering that Federated Department Stores, Inc., which he heads, last year did a $358,000,000 business through such stores as Bloomingdale's in New York, Filene's in Boston, Shillito's in Cincinnati, Abraham & Straus in Brooklyn, The Boston Store in Milwaukee and F. & R. Lazarus in Columbus, Ohio. At least 70 per cent of this represented sales to women. Yet, Fred admits, he still has a lot to learn about the workings of the female mind.

There is, for instance, the big question of what retailers call impulse buying. This has produced two bitterly opposed schools on the arrangement of store geography—the broken-field advocates and the wide-open-spacers. While husbands probably

won't believe it, the former insist most women go into a big store with the firm intention of simply picking up some specific item. A dress, a coat or a pair of shoes are the three top department-store sellers. To make you buy more, the broken-fielders employ architects, designers and, it's said, even psychologists to concoct mystic mazes of counters. These are so arranged that it's impossible for you to get anywhere in their stores without sighting innumerable displays of new, alluring "Daily Bargains," "Unadvertised Specials" and "Today Only Clearances."

Fred admits delay-and-sell may peddle impulse promotions. But, he insists, you'll probably grab a $3.50, just-marked-down bargain instead of continuing to the bag department, where, by the Lazarus plan, you'd be overwhelmed with so many bags in so many colors, fabrics, patterns and styles that you'd not only buy one but perhaps two at $4.94 and even $6.95. Additionally, because of his carefully thought-out placement of adjacent islands of related items, he trusts the buying mood will extend to the perfectly matched gloves just opposite and, a step away, the shoes most women buy with bags and gloves.

Selecting the open-field instead of the brokenspaces setup was one of the toughest questions which faced Mr. Fred when, not long ago, he decided to indulge in a fancy which department-store owners

PHOTOGRAPHY BY GEORGE BURNS

have long pipe-dreamed, but seldom attempted—a truly planned department store. Most United States stores, like Federated's older units, have grown up in fits and spurts. Few have dared leave expensive diggings, fearful that habit-nurtured customers might be lost en route. So they've expensively remodeled interiors, scooped new basements and makeshifted with annexes while limiting real modernization to relatively small suburban branches.

Fred, however, dreamed big and wanted something different. Almost his entire life, from knee pants on, has been spent in retailing. So, since Grandfather Simon opened the first Columbus, Ohio, store in 1851, have the lives of brothers Simon, Robert and Jeffrey, father Fred, Sr., Uncle Ralph and practically every other member of the clan known as the Lazari. Hence, when Fred bought the relatively modest $6,000,000-a-year operation known as Foley Brothers Dry Goods Company in Houston, Texas, shortened its name to Foley's and determined to build the first completely new store right from the basement up, a good many outsiders surmised it would turn out to be a glamorous, jet-propelled wonder. Foley's windowless walls, its helicopters going off the streamlined garage roof to make deliveries, and other similar publicity razzle-dazzle seemingly bore out that theory. Yet though Fred is a shrewd publicist, two generations have also instilled in him a fine sense of cost accounting. The result is that Foley's is different primarily because its $13,000,000 modernism has been necessary

Let the customers try it out—that's one of the principles Fred Lazarus operates under. The lady is cooking herself a titbit with a new type of iron.

Two hundred fifty dollars is the price of this white gown, being modeled in the presence of four shoppers and a mannequin in Foley's Crystal Room.

Foley's was the first department store built from the ground up in many years, and the new store was the talk of the nation. This magazine article heralds Fred Lazarus's innovative new store;

to achieve what older stores generally lack — the old-fashioned storekeeping aim which Fred sums up as: "Save nickels and dimes behind the scenes, conserve every piece of string and get an extra snap out of every rubber band — and you'll be counting the profits when the other boys are reaching for the red ink."

What Fred's store aims to do is to beat all comers, first in translating customer desires into specific merchandise — a woman's unresolved urge for something new for fall into a $28.40 pale-green dress; then bringing it to town before anybody else; next selling and getting it out to the customer with a minimum of effort, a maximum of speed and accuracy and at the lowest possible cost for both. This is no easy job. If goods arrive too far ahead of the trend, they have to wait around, eating up investment and precious space. If they come late, there's no sale. Timing is therefore the department store's first essential.

Every dress on the racks is checked weekly. If it hasn't been sold within two weeks, there are questions. If it's not out in three, there is action. It may be reduced; it may be shifted to another department. But it just won't be allowed to gather dust. "Ready-to-wear style is too fragile a bloom for any efficient store to keep on ice, even with air conditioning," Fred says. Men's fashions change less drastically than women's, yet no suit can remain in stock more than three months. Other ready-to-wear over five months is highly suspect and faces the heave-ho. A refrigerator can stay nine months, rugs slightly more, household goods a year. If, after advertising and proper display, an item still dies on the sales floor, Fred assumes there's something wrong with its style, fit, size or cost, in that order — never with the customers — and it gets no further promotion. "I'll try almost any idea once," he explains. "But when we've missed, bucking the trend is throwing good money after bad."

Lazarus' ultimate aim, of course, is to turn over goods as many times a year as possible, ringing up a profit on each transaction. Foley's volume has, in the four years since Fred took it over, almost quintupled to $29,000,000 yearly, and Fred thinks that's just the beginning. What makes his store different, however, is not volume — many stores are larger — but the way the cost of doing business is being attacked, so that the customer gets a lower price and Fred's stockholders a bigger profit. A good many outsiders figure that because department stores are so big their profits must *(Continued on Page 145)*

On the wall of his New York office Fred Lazarus, Jr., president of Federated Department Stores, has a huge picture of the revolutionary new Houston building, his thirteen-million-dollar dream store.

Inexpensive dresses are grouped by sizes instead of by style. The purchasers heartily approve.

You can leave your car in Foley's garage for an oil change, lubrication and wash, go into the store to shop, and by the time you get back to drive away, your parcels will be delivered to your automobile.

hence the title, "Mr. Fred's Dream Store."

This throng of shoppers waits patiently in front of Foley's on Main Street, ready for the doors to open.

Here is another view of crowd in front of store. Reporters from *Life*, *Newsweek*, *Vogue*, the Scripps Howard News Service, and officials from other retail stores from around the world joined thousands of curious Houstonians who jammed Main Street to get a peek at the new store when the board fence was lowered.

From left to right, Gov. William Hobby, Oveta Culp Hobby, and Celia Lazarus attend the opening. The gentleman with the mustache is unidentified.

Pictured, from left to right, are Celia Lazarus, famous Houston financier and commerce secretary Jesse Jones, and Marty Levine.

Foley's escalators were designed to operate at fast speeds in order to move large crowds. Back in the day, no one went downtown to shop without being dressed up. One teen mentioned how she was in the store wearing jeans after being at a school event when she ran into her mother's friends and became terribly embarrassed to be downtown in jeans.

Saleswomen wait patiently for customers as the opening-day patrons crowd in front of the jewelry department. So far it appears there aren't any buyers, just lookers.

Dressed in their "downtown" clothes, these ladies wait patiently for their turn in the shoe department.

The piece goods department was where shoppers came to buy material for home sewing. There definitely appears to be much more buying here and less "just looking."

Although not as popular today, aprons were a necessity for home cooks, as any period Hollywood movie will show.

A typical article shows various fashion leaders visiting Foley's. Balestra of Italy is shown with Foley model Betty Baseke. Madame Petin of Christian Dior was offering advice on coordinating hats with new outfits.

FASHION LEADERS VISIT FOLEY'S

BALESTRA

It was a delightful reunion for our fashion office and the Crystal room staff last week when Balestra returned to Foley's. This Italian designer is a great favorite with our customers and a charming ambassador of fashion. He is pictured here with Foley's model Betty Baseke during a rare lull between shows and consultations. Circle this collection on your must-see lists, it fills our windows and the Crystal Room.

MADAME PETIN OF CHRISTIAN DIOR

Touring fashion stores across America, the beautiful Anne Marie Petin spent last Wednesday in our millinery salon. A model with the House of Dior, her knowledgeable advise in coordinating a total look has made her a valuable envoy to customers and associates alike. The Dior Millinery collection is rich in color and texture, and ours alone in Houston.

A model walks the runway in a Foley's fashion show. These shows were typically held on the ready-to-wear fashion floor. The models also showed the clothes in the Azalea Terrace, where many female customers lunched.

Note the skirt lengths on this group of models and their gloves—something no lady would be without in those times.

The Shop of Originals was the custom hat department on the fourth floor and was also the largest women's hat department in Houston.

For many years, Foley's had a foreign fair that offered merchandise from around the world to customers. This picture shows a replica of the Trevi Fountain in Rome that graced the front of Foley's during the Italian Fair.

One of Foley's famous animated Christmas windows had a Cinderella theme. Citizens brought their children from Houston and surrounding areas each year to line up and look at Foley's Christmas windows. Many of today's adults remember the years their parents brought them to see these windows. (Photograph courtesy of the Bob Bailey Collection at the University of Texas.)

A group of men view the 50th anniversary window. In 1950, Foley's celebrated its 50th anniversary and offered a vision of what Houston would look like in the year 2000. Unfortunately, there still aren't elevated trains.

Christmastime featured a real, live Santa Claus in the window. (Photograph courtesy of the Bob Bailey Collection at the University of Texas.)

The 50th anniversary Vista window is pictured in all its glory.

Customers could choose from an abundant selection of purses when they shopped in the accessories department.

In November 1962, Foley's advertised a freezer and 150 pounds of food for only $298. Also note the advertisements to the side for contact paper, a Dishmaster, and Armstrong floor covering. Those were the days when Foley's carried everything; it was truly the place for one-stop shopping.

After Christmas each year, Foley's had day-after Christmas sales that brought the kind of crowds into the downtown store that can be associated with day-after-Thanksgiving sales today. Gift wrap and cards at half-off were a huge draw with customers running up the escalators to get the best merchandise. The men's shirt sale was another crowd favorite with huge assortments costing only $3.59.

Who wouldn't buy a Sealy mattress for $28? Today, it costs more than that to have it delivered.

This 1960 Christmas gift advertisement features dog beds, an aquarium, parakeets, and a brand-new Polaroid camera. There was also a 59-piece electric train set for only $13.

Four

COMMUNITY INVOLVEMENT

Starting as early as 1917, the management of Foley's believed strongly in the wisdom of having its executives and associates participate in community affairs. Not only did they play a major role in civic and charitable efforts of the community, but they also developed various programs for the employees at all levels. The end result of these efforts developed a strong bond among the weekly associates and the executives, and among the citizens of Houston who were their customers.

Early pictures show a group of Foley's employees, dressed in their Sunday best, in front of an interurban car—which was a 1920s version of a light rail—preparing to board for a daylong outing to Galveston. Another photograph shows Foley's semipro baseball team that was made up of employees and managed by my father, Lasker M. Meyer Sr.

As the years progressed, more and more events were added to the Foley calendar. Bowling, golf, and tennis tournaments were held year round. Bridge contests and social events were on the calendar weekly. Whether a truck driver, a salesperson, or the president, everyone participated.

Of major note was the Foley's Thanksgiving Day Parade. Various employees worked, on their own time, to make sure it was a success. They built floats, dressed in costumes as clowns, or supervised the Boy Scouts holding the inflated balloons in high winds. It was a major event in Houston, and its citizens turned out by the thousands. Pictures show crowds of parents and children filling the sidewalks and overflowing into the street. The parade ended in front of Foley's downtown store where Santa descended from his float and climbed a ladder to the marquis over the main entrance to an elaborate scene that was built by the display department. Every band and high school girls drill team from Houston and surrounding areas participated. After the parade, from Thanksgiving to Christmas, families from all over the area came to the downtown store to view the Christmas windows that were full of animated toys and exhibits. It was a major family event in Houston and is remembered fondly by all who participated.

Equally as important is the part that Foley's played in civic activities. Although George Cohen was an important and active member of the community, Leopold Meyer, his brother-in-law, was the most active in civic affairs. He was one of the seven founding members of the Houston Community Chest (later the United Way), was a founder and president of the Houston Music Association, and founded and served as president of the 100 Club and the Houston Crime Commission. The 100 Club supports the officers and their families of various police entities in the metropolitan Houston area. Meyer was president of the Houston Horse Show Association for 25 years when its main effort was to fund the new Texas Children's Hospital. He was president of the Texas Children's Hospital until his death, and a major wing of the hospital is named after him.

In the Federated Department Store years, members of management at all levels were equally active in the community. Foley's took a leadership position, both financially and through volunteering with the United Way of Houston, with members of management serving as annual fund chairmen. Both Milton Berman and Stewart Orton were active in the symphony, ballet, contemporary art museum, and museum of fine arts. Other groups that benefited from Foley's participation included the chamber of commerce, the Houston Job Training Program, Harris County Children's Protective Service, Alley Theater, Wortham Theater, Forum Club, and Central Houston.

Foley's not only participated through volunteer activities but also financially and through its advertising. The archives are filled with letters of appreciation from civic leaders and plain citizens thanking Foley's for aiding their causes. Some were from major civic groups such as the symphony or the Fat Stock Show and Rodeo but others were from tiny PTA groups in towns as far away as a hundred miles. In the pre-Federated Department Stores years, Foley's had a variety group that performed in its auditorium each week and that traveled to the many small towns of Texas to perform at various community fundraisers.

It was through all these efforts that Foley's became "Houston's Store."

Foley's planned activities for employees started early in the 1920s. This photograph is of an employee outing taken on the interurban from Houston to Galveston.

A group of employees played on Foley's semiprofessional baseball team in the 1920s. The manager in the suit and straw hat is Lasker M. Meyer Sr.

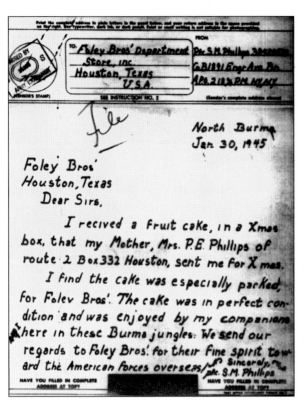

A letter from a soldier in North Burma, dated 1945, stated that he had received a fruitcake in perfect condition sent by his mother from Foley's. He thanks Foley's "for their fine spirit towards the American Forces overseas." This letter was on a form specifically provided by the armed services to allow its servicemen to communicate with those at home.

North Burma
Jan 30, 1945

Foley Bros'
Houston, Texas
Dear Sirs,

I recived a fruit cake, in a Xmas box, that my Mother, Mrs. P.E. Phillips of route 2 Box 332 Houston, sent me for X mas.
I find the cake was especially packed for Foley Bros'. The cake was in perfect condition and was enjoyed by my companions here in these Burma jungles. We send our regards to Foley Bros' for their fine spirit toward the American forces overseas.
Sincerely,
pfc. S.M. Phillips

This letter from an officer of the PTA at Horace Mann Junior High School in Goose Creek, Texas, is an example of the many letters sent to Foley's from all over the state. This particular one thanked the store for providing the entertainment of Foley's Town Hall Show at a benefit for the school.

309 W. Pierce ave,
Goose, Creek, Texas
May 15, 1941.

Dear Mitzie,
This is to inform you that our proceeds from your Town Hall Show in the Horace Mann School amounted to $50.60. Foley Brothers are to be commended for making it possible for the neighboring communities to enjoy such a fine show. Thank you for a delightful evening; and we shall look forward to your coming again next season.
Sincerely,
Mrs. R.M. Wedgeworth, Sec'y
Horace Mann P.T.A.
Goose Creek

60

This letter from an employee of the *Houston Defender*, a newspaper for the African American community, thanks Foley's for extending credit to him during a period of difficulty. It was typical for management to be willing to work with their customers and keep them happy.

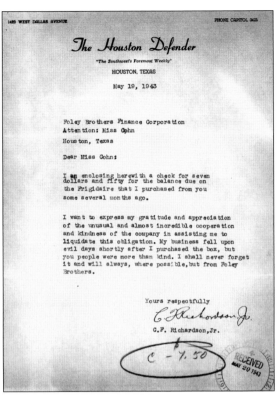

1425 WEST DALLAS AVENUE   PHONE CAPITOL 0425

The Houston Defender
"The Southwest's Foremost Weekly"
HOUSTON, TEXAS

May 19, 1943

Foley Brothers Finance Corporation
Attention: Miss Cohn
Houston, Texas

Dear Miss Cohn:

I am enclosing herewith a check for seven dollars and fifty for the balance due on the Frigidaire that I purchased from you some several months ago.

I want to express my gratitude and appreciation of the unusual and almost incredible cooperation and kindness of the company in assisting me to liquidate this obligation. My business fell upon evil days shortly after I purchased the box, but you people were more than kind. I shall never forget it and will always, where possible, but from Foley Brothers.

Yours respectfully

C.F. Richardson, Jr.

RECEIVED
MAY 20 1943

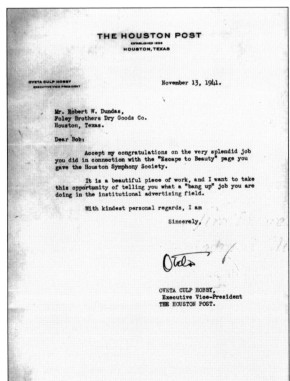

THE HOUSTON POST
ESTABLISHED 1896
HOUSTON, TEXAS

OVETA CULP HOBBY
EXECUTIVE VICE PRESIDENT   November 13, 1941.

Mr. Robert W. Dundas,
Foley Brothers Dry Goods Co.
Houston, Texas.

Dear Bob:

Accept my congratulations on the very splendid job you did in connection with the "Escape to Beauty" page you gave the Houston Symphony Society.

It is a beautiful piece of work, and I want to take this opportunity of telling you what a "bang up" job you are doing in the institutional advertising field.

With kindest personal regards, I am

Sincerely,

Oveta

OVETA CULP HOBBY,
Executive Vice-President
THE HOUSTON POST.

This letter from Oveta Culp Hobby thanks Foley's for an advertisement supporting the Houston Symphony Society. Mrs. Hobby, the wife of the governor of Texas, was the executive vice president of the *Houston Post* and during World War II was head of the Women's Army Corps.

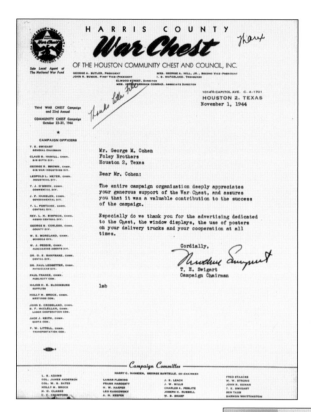

A letter from the War Chest, a division of the Houston Community Chest (now known as United Way) thanks Foley's for efforts made to ensure the success of their campaign during World War II.

This letter from the Houston Fat Stock Show thanks Foley's for an advertisement promoting the show. All of these letters were selected to show a cross-section of the type of support Foley's provided Houston and the surrounding communities. Although these letters are mostly dated during the decade of the 1940s, the letters in Foley's archives cover 60 years of community involvement.

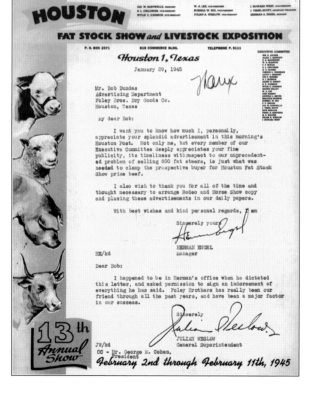

This advertisement, dated Thursday, November 26, 1960, was for the Christmas season. This was before stores felt the need to advertise for after-Thanksgiving promotions to generate business.

This advertisement from 1960 promotes "Foley's Giant Christmas Parade, Thanksgiving Day" The inset map shows the parade route.

These two pictures show the crowd of Houstonians who jammed the streets along the entire route of the parade.

The first Foley's Thanksgiving Day Parade took place November 22, 1951, with Mayor Oscar Holcombe, a Marine color guard, and the Elk Cadets drum and bugle corps leading the way. Marvin Stalarow had designed the window displays for Foley's and helped organize the event. Each year, Boy Scouts troops worked in the parade controlling the inflated floats, some on the street, some in the air. In this photograph, scouts are dressed as clowns as they pull a large duck float.

This float shows Dumbo, a popular comic character at that time, on a motorized float. Motorized floats were pulled by cars that were decorated as part of the float.

Ninfa Lorenzo, a popular Mexican restaurant owner and an icon of not only the Hispanic community, but the entire city, took part in the parade in a decorated car.

Members of the Johnson County Sheriff's Posse carry Confederate flags, which were still politically correct at that time.

Roy Rogers, the most famous movie cowboy of his time, is pictured on his horse, Trigger.

Shown here are some of the various floats and participants that were featured in the Foley's Thanksgiving Day Parade.

Cowboys, riding on beautiful silver-trimmed saddles, represent members of the many trail rides that came to Houston for the Fat Stock Show and Rodeo.

Shown here are students from the Evergreen Chinese School. Every ethnic group in the city at that time participated in the Foley's Thanksgiving Day Parade.

The Booker T. Washington High School marching band performs with its baton twirlers. It was one of the most famous high school marching bands in the city.

A girls' group representing a dance school participates in Foley's famous and well-attended Foley's Thanksgiving Day Parade.

Large crowds watch as a large Thanksgiving turkey float and a local marching band pass by during the parade.

Pictured here is a Christmas float with elves portrayed by Lisa Bernell (left) and Susan Meyer. It was common for members of Foley's associates' families to take part in the parade.

The Santa Claus float was always the last float in Foley's Thanksgiving Day Parade. The float stopped on Main Street in front of Foley's where Santa climbed up the ladder to his toyshop.

Santa Claus climbs up the ladder to his toyshop in front of Foley's main entrance as one of the final spectacles of the annual Foley's Thanksgiving Day Parade.

WAREHOUSE WHISTLES

—By Angelina Heintz

Aesop Fable No. 3:

HAPPY IS THE MAN WHO LEARNS FROM THE MISFORTUNES OF OTHERS.

Since this is my first article to the Port-Foley-O (and I don't know just what to say), but I guess I could introduce Mr. Davis, who is now with the Delivery Department. Happy to have you, Thurman, as an associate in our organization. Just don't let the packages and routes confuse you.

Gee! Is our Cafeteria doing O. K. Thanks, Vera, the spaghetti and meat "ball" was good.

The Appliance Service Department sure has been wheeling and dealing, with Mr. Margulies as their new manager, "good luck Jerry," and Mr. Abbott back with the department.

We certainly do miss Mr. Hilburn, especially his friendly smile when he says good morning. He has been sick for a few days.

Mr. Parnell sure does stay busy, pulling tags off of baby beds and baby bassinettes. That's O. K. Eugene, I really don't mind mailing tags to the infant department, especially when I am all ready to go home.

Last, but not least, I must say a word or two about the Drapery Department. Girls, you are doing a swell job. The furniture you cover and make slip covers for looks O. K. to me.

Only fools answer all questions. Why did the little moron's girl friend make him a sweater of banana peels? (So he would have something to slip on.)

This week "Commendation Award" goes to T. B. Stephenson for his whole-hearted co-operation, and fine spirit in repairing damage to the home of one of our customers.

(Editor's note: We tried to secure Mr. Stephenson's photograph, but did not make connections for this issue.)

WELCOME TO FOLEY'S

MRS. VIRGINIA V. HINTON, was appointed Assistant Department Manager of Leather goods, Main Floor, on February 3rd, 1947. Born in Georgia, she has lived in Houston for seven years and was formerly with Sweeny's and Corrigan's Jewelry Companies. She lists as among her main hobbies the collecting of gem stones, of which she has a very large and unusual collection. Foley's welcome mat is out to you, Mrs. Hinton.

Associates At Play

MEN'S BOWLING LEAGUE RESULTS

Friday, February 14th:

Margulies team won two and lost one to Erickson; Whigham won two and lost one to Abel; Kaufman won two and lost one to Rivers; Coppinger won all three games from Boen.

Meeks rolled high individual game with 197, and high individual series with 495. Boen was second with a high game of 188 and 491 for individual series.

Coppinger was high with high team game when they rolled 761, and high team series with 2134. Here are the standings of the league through February 14th, 1947: High individual game, Abel, 245; high individual series, Abel, 617; high team game, Coppinger, 834; high team series, Coppinger, 2231.

FIRST FLOOR FANFARE

—By Lillian Uselton

Here is your first floor reporter again, after missing the deadline last issue.

The busiest department on the main floor, at this writing, is the Square in front of the elevators, where the Valentines were on display.

We will miss Mr. Albertson of the Luggage Department, who will be absent while recovering from a minor operation on Valentine's Day. Hurry back, Mr. Albertson.

Miss Collen Stalnaker, of the Book Department, has left the store to join her family in Orange, Texas, where her father was transferred in his work.

We welcome Mrs. Sanford Hopkins as a regular associate, instead of an extra, in the Book Department.

We're sorry to hear of Mrs. Proebstle's (of the Bag Department) absence from the store, due to a fall from a ladder. We trust that you will soon be back with us, Mrs. Proebstle.

In the above photo are members of River's team in the Foley Bros. Men's Bowling League. They are, from left to right, **PATTERSON, LEVY, RIVERS, CASTLEBERRY** and **LEE.**

BASEMENT BANTER

—By Georgia Huntington

A breakfast and a stork shower was given in the Cafeteria Thursday morning, February 13th, for Mrs. Ruth Allen of the Basement Buyer's Office. She received some lovely gifts and everyone had a lovely time.

Girls' and Infants' Wear associates express their deepest sympathy to Lolly Romera upon the death of her sister-in-law.

The Sportswear Department has a new associate, Mrs. Josephine Weekly, formerly of the Toy Department. Welcome to the family, Josephine.

Overheard in the Basement: "No, thank you, I don't need any help, I haven't been to town in a long time and am just looking around." Another one: "I don't know what size slip she wears but it is the same size as the girl's next door."

BASKET BALL

The Colored Basket Ball Team is really "going down the line" after losing two straight games at the start of the season. They have come from behind to take three in a row. Foley's team beat the highly favored Hester House Five with a score of 58 to 45 to start their winning streak. They then came back to take the measure of the Tyler Barber College and the Invaders.

The team is now in fifth place in the City League and hopes to be on top when the season ends.

— Henry Watson, Reporter.

This page taken from the *port*Foley*o* shows some of the activities associates enjoyed.

73

The Houston Press

Index

VOL. 46   NO. 269   HOUSTON, TEXAS, MONDAY, AUG. 6, 1956   Phones   FIVE CENTS

Market Hit by Sharp Break

See S
In C

BOMB PLOT AT DOWNTOWI
STORE FOILED! FBI JAILS

$50,000 Extortion Note to Officials; Dummy Is Plantec

FBI Arrested These Men

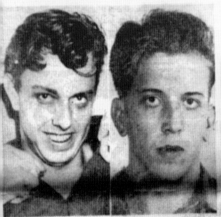

DONALD ROY QUINN   KENNETH WAYNE QUINN

FBI Checked This Car

Sobbing Mother Puts Blame on Oldest Son

Two brothers, arrested by FBI agen
night, were charged today with trying
lect $50,000 by threatening to plant a b
a downtown store.

A third man was arrested with them, but
charged.

The extortionists demanded the $50,000 in

Praises the FBI

Max Levine, president and general manager of
said:

"Full credit for solving this case goes to the
"Our hats are off to them for the swif
thorough job they did in apprehending the o
ers. And we are deeply grateful as citizens
this efficient organization stands ready with
and protection when it is needed."

$1 to $100 denomination. The Press learned,
sisted that at least $10,000 be in $1 bills.

The men were arrested at 9:30 last night in
block of N. Main and were booked in county
a.m. today.

The extortion plot was against Foley's.

The arrests came after a store official re
anonymous letter saying a d u m m y bomb
placed and that a real one would be set if th
was not paid.

Charged before U. S. Commissioner Billy Co

DONALD ROY QU
2010 Chate. He is a br
and gave his occupa
furniture mover.
KENNETH WAYN

Bundle Would

In 1956, the *Houston Press* reported that two young men phoned to claim they had planted a bomb inside Foley's. After a thorough inspection, it was discovered that no bomb existed.

Five

BRANCH EXPANSION

Sometime in late 1959, the decision to open Foley's first branch store was made. Expansion into the suburbs was a relatively new retail development, and only a few of the Federated Department Stores had branches, namely Abraham & Straus, Burdines, and Shillito's. A Houston developer, Frank Sharp, had built a residential community 13 miles from downtown bordering on a soon-to-be-built freeway. He then began planning for an enclosed, air-conditioned shopping center—the first of its kind in Houston and, perhaps, in the United States.

Naturally, Sharp's first thought was of Foley's. After a great deal of area research by Federated Department Stores and bargaining with Sharp, the agreement was signed. In order to get his shopping center under way Sharp agreed to give Federated Department Stores the ground and parking area the store would be built upon and also to pay the cost of the store's construction! This enabled him to go to other retailers—such as Montgomery Ward, which anchored the other end of the mall, S.S. Kresge and Battelstein's in the middle, and other specialty stores—and get their agreement to join the center. Hence, Houston's first air-conditioned suburban shopping center was born.

Shortly after the decision to build the first branch was made, the next step was figuring out who would manage it. Only one current Foley's executive had experience running a small store in the suburbs—Lasker Meyer. He was told he would be manager but that he could not disclose that information until a later date. It turned out that he had to sit on that secret for more than six months. Bill Kaplan, his immediate supervisor and divisional merchandise manager, told him that he was making a big mistake and he should stay a buyer as he could eventually become a divisional manager like Kaplan was. It did not take Meyer long to disregard that advice.

Eventually, Meyer's promotion was announced and Charles Luft and Meyer went to New York to meet with the same interior designer who had designed the downtown Foley's store. Construction was underway and Meyer spent most of his time working with management deciding who would be a member of the management team. The store's opening was scheduled for September 1961.

Days before the opening of Foley's and the rest of the Sharpstown center, Hurricane Carla hit Houston. Most of the management team spent the night in the store making sure no major damage occurred. Needless to say, Meyer's wife spent many years reminding him that he spent the night protecting the store while she was home with their two young daughters.

Foley's, and the entire shopping center, was an immediate success. There was no competition in the most populous area of the city other than what existed in the center itself and the few stores in the Rice Village shopping center. The most serious problem Foley's faced was an internal one. Max Levine was anxious to preserve the volume in the downtown store and not have its volume transferred to Sharpstown, so he told the merchandising organization that they were responsible for merchandising downtown and protecting its volume. Sharpstown's success was beyond expectations and the most important task the Sharpstown management organization had was to get enough merchandise from the downtown buyers to keep the sales increase going. This set up a conflict situation and a great deal of Meyer's effort was spent putting pressure on the merchandising organization to fill the store's requirements. They kept records of every request made for merchandise and when those requests went unfilled they had to go up the chain of command and exert pressure. Eventually, most of the buyers and merchandise managers came to understand that Sharpstown's growth was in their best interest but there were some holdouts that caused continual conflict.

Sharpstown's growth continued at a rapid rate. Within several years it was the most profitable branch store of Federated Department Stores. Foley's management made the decision to open a second branch store that was smaller than Sharpstown and in a different demographic area. Pasadena, a separate community with its own mayor and city council, was an industrial area along the ship channel where most of the oil refineries and chemical plants were located. The population was mostly blue collar but was well paid. The decision was made to open a store there as a branch of Foley's downtown Basement Store with centrally located cash register checkout stations. It opened on August 25, 1962, with Z.M. "Click" Eisenberg moving from a divisional sales manager position at Sharpstown to being the Pasadena store's first manager.

Customer response was immediate. Unlike Sharpstown, it was mostly bad. Customers had come in expecting to find a mini-Sharpstown with merchandise similar to that carried in the downtown store. When they saw the merchandise was mostly low-end from the Basement Store and the cash register lineup, they were outraged. Even though they were blue collar, the customers felt that Foley's management was treating them as second-class citizens. Although the Pasadena store had been copied from another Federated Department Stores branch in Ohio, the decision was quickly made to change the store. The merchandise mix was changed to more closely match Sharpstown's and the cash registers were moved to the individual departments, just as they were in other Foley's stores. Bad feelings on the part of the customers disappeared, and Pasadena began its successful growth.

In spite of the success of Sharpstown and Pasadena and the continued growth of Foley's due to the growth of metropolitan Houston, all was not well with Foley's. Several top-level merchandise organization appointments severely affected the morale of the company. This did not go unnoticed by Federated Department Stores management. The decision was made to make Max Levine chairman of the board and to bring in Milton S. Berman as president. Berman came from Abraham & Straus in Brooklyn, where he was the vice president and general merchandise manager. The appointment was announced on February 15, 1964, and he arrived within a month. Shortly afterward, on March 24, 1964, it was announced that Stewart Orton would join Berman in the typical two-man management structure that Federated Department Stores used. Orton was vice president and general merchandise manager in charge of merchandising and publicity. Within two years, Levine retired, Berman became chairman and chief executive officer, and Orton became president.

While Lasker Meyer was manager of the Sharpstown store, he began working with Richard Roeder on the design of two twin stores, Northwest and Almeda-Genoa. Roeder had once been in charge of Foley's planning department, but had left to start his very successful store planning organization, Richard Roeder and Associates. Roeder came up with a plan that was unique in department store design. Normally, stores were designed with aisles crossing both vertically and horizontally, and different types of merchandise were adjacent to each other. In an entirely new approach, Roeder designed a store that was a group of stores within a store. On the first floor were a feminine apparel store, a men's store, a children's store, and a feminine accessory and cosmetic store. The balance of the departments (mainly for the home) were located in a similar configuration on the second floor. The only aisle was a "racetrack" which circled the store. Usually there were four entrances so the customer could park near the "store" they wished to visit, but if they wanted to go to another store within a store they would have to go on the "racetrack," passing and being exposed to other merchandise along the way. At first, Federated Department Stores management was resistant to this innovation but the design was eventually approved. This became the format for all Foley's stores in succeeding years.

Milt Berman and Stew Orton were a dynamic team. They insisted on being called by their first names by other executives, which was a distinct difference from the formal "Mr. Levine" years. They properly assessed the potential of the growth of Houston and the part that Foley's would play in it. In January 1966, Berman appointed Lasker Meyer vice president in charge of branch development. Although he was responsible for the development of the branch stores and the selection of the executives to staff them, the managers reported directly to Orton. Berman was a great believer in simple management structures and did not want another level between the branch managers and Orton.

In September 1966, the 200,000-square-foot Almeda-Genoa branch opened, anchoring a major shopping center with J.C. Penney's at the other end. It serviced the southeast section of Houston and reached as far as Galveston and Texas City.

In November of that year, the first of Sharpstown's three expansions was announced.

On July 31, 1967, Almeda-Genoa's twin, Northwest, opened. Within two years Foley's had added 500,000 square feet of selling space.

Both of these stores were immediately successful, following the Sharpstown store's pattern. Their success led to the first major strategic blunder that Foley's made in their expansion strategy. Right in the geographic center between Sharpstown and Northwest, a new development was being formed on the corner of Westheimer Road and Post Oak Boulevard by the Hines Interests that was named "the Galleria" after the famous center of the same name in Milan, Italy. The center was unique in that it had a major ice-skating rink on its lower level and was anchored at its eastern end by a major Neiman-Marcus specialty store. Across the street to the east was a major, full-line Joske's, and across the street to the north was a new Sakowitz store. Obviously, the Hines Interests organization wanted Foley's to join the mall, but Federated Department Stores research indicated that the transfer of volume from the Sharpstown and Northwest stores would seriously affect their volume and profit. Therefore, the first of several decisions, then and in the future, was made not to build a store in that mall. None of Foley's management foresaw the fact that the Galleria area would become the major shopping area, replacing downtown. It was not until many years later, after passing up multiple opportunities that were filled by Lord & Taylor and Macy's, that Foley's eventually built a store in the Galleria. Sales at Sharpstown and Northwest diminished due to demographic changes and also because additional Foley's stores were built, effectively transferring sales. In 2009, both the Sharpstown and Northwest stores closed.

In keeping with the growth of the Houston metropolitan area, Foley's expanded rapidly. In February 1974, Foley's opened its Memorial City store, located in the fast-growing and affluent west part of Houston. In August 1986, the Greenspoint store opened in the North area. Proof of the growth of Houston and Foley's lies in the fact that every store from Sharpstown to Greenspoint was expanded shortly after it was built, some of them more than once.

Susan Meyer, Lasker Meyer's daughter, attended the University of Texas in Austin. Each trip home was accompanied by a list of complaints regarding the lack of a Foley's store in Austin. Meyer related her complains to Milton Berman and Stewart Orton, and finally the group accompanied by Federated Department Stores area research experts visited Austin and its major mall, Highland. Within a short while, Foley's first store outside of Houston opened, with Bob Oliver as manager.

In 1980, Foley's built a store in San Jacinto Mall in Baytown, Texas. The store's customer mix was similar to Pasadena but the actual store itself resembled the newest of Foley's stores, only smaller.

In June 1980, Foley's announced plans to build three stores in San Antonio, Texas, the first of which was in San Antonio's largest mall, Northstar. Foley's first female store manager, Teresa Byrd, was appointed and Bob Oliver became the regional vice president over all of Foley's remote stores.

Northstar, like most of the Houston and Austin stores, was an immediate success, with customers not only from San Antonio but many from south of the Texas border.

In September 1981, the Willowbrook store in Houston's fast-growing northwest area was opened, followed six months later by the second store in Austin in Barton Creek Mall. Six months later, the West Oaks store in far west Houston opened. Six months later, the second San Antonio store in Ingram Park opened. Opening four stores, one every six months, was a major accomplishment for the Foley organization, while still achieving strong growth in existing stores.

The year 1984 saw the opening of two more stores, Deerbrook in Humble, Texas, (a suburb of northeast Houston) and A&M Post Oak in College Station, Texas, that served the community of Texas A&M University. A small but significant effort by Foley's to become part of the community was the fact that the sign on the store was in maroon, Texas A&M University's color, which was a deviation from the signs on all other Foley's stores. Finally, in 1987, a store opened in Staples Mall in Corpus Christi, Texas. This was the last store opened by Foley's until its merger with Sanger-Harris in the spring of 1987.

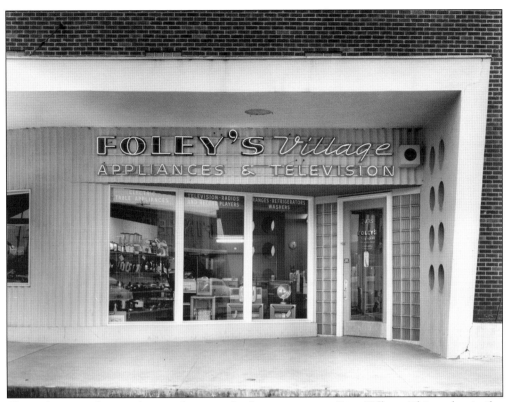

Shown here is a freestanding appliance and television store in Rice Village. This and a similar store in Palm Center on Houston's south side were the first efforts to attract suburban customers. Both were closed shortly after the opening of Foley's full-line branch in Sharpstown.

A montage on the cover of a 1986 issue of *port*Foley*o* shows all of Foley's branches from 1961 to 1987.

The Sharpstown store, Foley's first full-line branch, opened in 1961. It was an immediate success and underwent three separate expansions.

"There's No Business . . .

Like Our Business"

STAGE

Max Levine, President of Foley's and Lasker Meyer, Sharpstown Manager, cut the ribbon which marked the "grand opening" of Foley's Sharpstown Store.

This lovely new addition to the Foley Family covers 170,000 square feet in Sharpstown Center. The light spacious interior features numerous unique portions: Massive sliding glass panels, an illuminated escalator, brightly colored columns and whimsical murals, a "Fashion Oval" composed of seven display platforms, removable panels that change with the seasons and many other Foley Firsts. The gleaming exterior of riverbed stone and white painted brick, surrounded by stately oak trees and tropical greenery, sets the stage for the beauty inside.

Foley's Sharpstown Store is a fine example of the growth and progress which has taken place in Foley's Sixty One-derful Years.

The images accompanying this brief article show the mall entrance of the Sharpstown store.

This photograph shows the ground-breaking for the store in Pasadena, Texas. This was Foley's second branch and though it was much smaller than the Sharpstown store it underwent expansion due to success.

The Foley's store in Pasadena is pictured soon after it was completed on August 25, 1962. This was the second branch store for Foley's after Sharpstown. Initially, Foley's modeled the store after another branch store Federated opened in Ohio. However, Pasadena customers were unhappy with low-end merchandise, and Foley's quickly changed the store to more closely match Sharpstown's.

Pictured here is the ground-breaking of the Almeda-Genoa store, located on the Gulf Freeway. Established in the fall of 1966, it was one of two twin stores with an interior design and traffic pattern that retained Foley's signature store format.

This issue of the *port*Foley*o* shows the twin store, Northwest, and its initial management. As the name indicated, it served the northwest quadrant of Houston for years until development outboard was needed.

VOLUME 29, NUMBER 7   Foley's Store Newspaper   FEBRUARY 15, 1974

Memorial City Opens Its Doors On Monday

The eagerly awaited opening of the Memorial City Foley's is here... Monday, Tuesday and Wednesday are Courtesy Days, and Thursday, Feb. 21 at 9:45 a.m. will be the Grand Opening ceremonies for the newly-completed section of the shopping center that includes Foley's. Next week's issue will be a special edition about the new store, its people and its operations. Don't miss it!

The Memorial City store opened in February 1974 in Houston's affluent west side. This was a variation on past designs in that it was only on one floor. In subsequent years the size was doubled, making it the largest one-floor store in the state.

Shown here is the Greenspoint store in far north Houston. It was so successful that expansion planning started within a year after it opened.

The Highland Mall store in Austin, Texas, was Foley's first venture into a city outside of the metropolitan Houston area. It opened in July 1979. (Photograph by Patti Francis.)

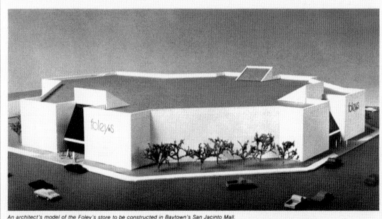

An architect's model of the Foley's store to be constructed in Baytown's San Jacinto Mall.

The San Jacinto Mall in Baytown, Texas, was an area similar to Pasadena with a high concentration of oil refineries. It was so named because it was near the San Jacinto battlefield and monument where the battle for Texas independence from Mexico was won.

Baytown's San Jacinto Mall will be site of next Foley's

150,000 square foot facility will be eighth full-line store in Houston area

Foley's has announced plans for a Baytown store to open in 1981.

The new 150,000 square foot facility will be one of the anchors of the upcoming San Jacinto Mall, under development at the corner of Interstate 10 and Garth Road, by Paul Broadhead and Associates, of Meridian, Mississippi. Previously announced anchors will be Sears, Montgomery Ward and JC Penney.

The new Baytown unit will be the eighth full-line Foley's in the Houston metropolitan area.

In making this announcement, Stewart

Orton, chairman, asserted, "The 1980's will continue to challenge retailers to keep pace with the explosive growth of the region. We intend to go forward into this new decade well-prepared to meet that challenge."

Lasker Meyer, president, added, "The Baytown addition is a significant step in the completion of our long-range commitment to growth and expansion. With our new Highland Mall store which opened last month in Austin, and this new Baytown facility, Foley's will be operating 10 selling units by the end of 1981."

North Star in San Antonio, Texas, was Foley's first store in the major mall in that city that not only served the citizens of the city but also many visitors from Mexico and South and Central America. It opened in the summer of 1981 and was enlarged shortly afterward. Its opening was announced as part of a three-store strategy for the city of San Antonio.

Barton Creek, Foley's second store in Austin, opened in March 1982.

Six

INTEGRATION

The decade of the 1960s was a period of conflict all over the United States as various states and communities wrestled with the issue of racial integration. As civil rights protests escalated, there were violent clashes in southern states and also in some degree in northern states as busing to integrate schools and other issues such as segregated facilities and Jim Crow laws were challenged.

In Houston, on March 4, 1960, a group of 13 courageous students from Texas Southern University, an African American college, joined hands and began their march to the Weingarten grocery store near the campus. They were led by Eldrewey Stearns, who strategized the entire effort. They sat down at the lunch counter but were not served. They sat for hours. The lunch counter closed. They still stayed. The next day, the local media were filled with accounts of this small but orderly demonstration.

More and more "sit-ins," as they were called, occurred. Foley's first-floor luncheonette had sit-ins daily. It too was closed. In addition, students and their supporters picketed outside Foley's asking for the end of segregation in return for their patronage to the store.

While many white citizens believed in the justification of the students' efforts, an equal number did not. An impasse occurred. Bob Dundas, Foley's senior vice president for advertising and publicity, was concerned. Dundas remembered the race riots of 1917 in Houston when African American troops stationed at Camp Logan (now Memorial Park, named for those who were killed) rioted because of treatment by Houston police. Dundas was determined that these riots would not reoccur. He contacted his counterpart at Rich's Department Store in Atlanta to find out how he had handled the situation.

Dundas met with John T. Jones of the *Houston Chronicle* and Hobart Taylor of the African American community and developed a strategy to integrate Houston. He got agreement that in the last week of August, 70 lunch counters would integrate peacefully. They did, and there was not one mention of it in Houston newspapers in spite of the fact that it was a nationally known event. Most citizens did not know it had taken place.

Dundas's skill as a negotiator and the fact that Foley's was by far the largest advertiser in the newspapers accomplished this blackout of the news. To say that this was controversial is an understatement, but due to his efforts and the small group working with him, Houston was integrated with no conflict. Shortly afterwards, agreement was reached to integrate movie theaters and hotels. This was partly due to the fact that Roy Hofheinz and the county were building the Astrodome for a major league baseball club and knew that some teams would not come with African American players to a Jim Crow town.

When Foley's downtown store was built, it had lunch counters, a full-service tearoom, and the Men's Grill on the second floor located behind the men's clothing department. When women's groups all over the country began demanding equal rights, the Houston group decided that the Men's Grill should be integrated. Small groups with signs began marching through the grill for days, demanding equal service. Foley's gave in, and it was then called "the Grill."

Worth noting is that Foley's in Houston was a leader in hiring members of the African American community, both in support functions behind the scenes and as salespeople. It also led in giving credit privileges to African American customers. This developed a loyalty to Foley's that equaled that among whites.

Not an integration issue, but of great importance, was the battle between retail interests in Texas over the so-called "blue laws." These laws prevented the opening of any kind of retail establishment seven days a week. The law had been carefully crafted because similar laws in other states had been declared unconstitutional by the courts. Texas law was different in that the retailer could decide whether to stay open either Saturday or Sunday, but not both. The blue laws were passed under the guise of a religious issue and although they were supported by the religious community, they were in fact a battle between different retail groups who either wanted to only operate six days a week or those who wanted to be open seven days. On one side were established retailers, such as Foley's, and on the other were retailers such as automobile dealers, discount stores, and, notably, Academy Sporting Goods, which felt that its sportsmen customers should be able to shop both Saturday and Sunday. Milton Berman, Foley's chairman, with a legal team and lobbyist, was a major player in trying to keep the laws enforced. Eventually, changing demographics among the retailers and their customers won out, and Houston and other Texas retailers are now open seven days and six nights a week. This has been carried to an extreme with stores being open on major holidays like the Fourth of July and Memorial Day, and only Christmas, Thanksgiving, and Easter remaining when most, but not all, retail establishments close. This extension of days and hours, while serving some customers, had the effect of reducing the amount of volume done per hour open, which then caused stores to rely on fewer employees or less experienced ones. This, in fact, reduced customer service to the level that it is today. Store hours have been carried out to such a ridiculous extreme that some stores open as early as 4:00 a.m. on major sales days in order to try to get a jump on the competition.

To: Mr. Dundas   9/10/58

RE: First Floor Soda Fountain - Sit Down Case.

On Monday, September 8th, at about 4:20 p.m., four (4) colored
women -
          - Mrs. Clara Ewing   4725 Meadow Park
          - Mrs. Lou VonDaniel   2604 Drew
          - Mrs. Dorothy L. Mitchel   3203 Windburn
          - Mrs. L. R. Goldberg   3233 Tuam (CA8-4249) — (Husband writes
                                                              [feminide CC
walked into our 1st. floor Soda Fountain, seated themselves
at the counter and waited to be served. As per instructions,
the Restaurant Manager called for assistance. Mr. Stephenson
was first to arrive - he greeted the women and after a ten
minute discussion they agreed to accompany him to our 7th
floor restaurant. Andy Cipriani advised Mr. Luft who broke
into a meeting I was having and I made my way to 7th floor
and made my presence evident to Mr. Stephenson. At about
5:00 p.m., he excused himself, came out to the corridor and
told me that he was not getting anywhere and would I take
over.

I introduced myself to the women who had been seated and
had been served coffee and cokes. They wanted to speak
to Mr. Levine and I asked if I could help, then we started,
an hour and one-half of discussion, criticism and requests
bordering on demand, with some threat for colored eating
facilities, and additional toilet rooms.

This group was evidently well schooled. They kept up a
constant chatter - when one would stop the other would
pick up. As and when I offerred explanation or comments
they would attempt to cut me short.

As customers in the store, they stated we had no hesitation
to take their money across the counter, yet we would not allow
them the privilege of dining at Foley's. The nations enemies
were welcome to come into the store and have total privileges
and yet the colored who fought for the nation and their
families were being repaid by the unfair barrier that has
been established.

I attempted to counter and offer logical explanation as per
our discussion prior to your leaving on vacation. I am not
sure that we gained anything but time. After an hour and one-
half they evidently tired. They want to hear from me and I
told them that I would contact Mrs. Goldberg at some later date.
They want to attend our Board of Directors meeting to personally
present their case.

This inter-store memo sent to Robert Dundas, senior vice president for publicity and public affairs, was the first indication that Foley's would be involved in integration efforts taking place in the city.

In summary, I believe -

They willingly accompanied Mr. Stephenson to the
7th floor because they did not know that we had
such a restaurant facility. This was not covered
in their prior schooling and they went ahead, not
knowing what tack to take. Once they entered the
7th floor restaurant they were quick to run it
down - its location, appearance, size and lack of
signing.

They wanted us to provide restaruant facilities
for colored. Their request was not for integration
of our present restaruants but one for colored.
Addition of our Picnic Patio was mentioned often.
We added another for the white customers even though
we had several already in existence. Why didn't we
consider their needs.

As for toilet rooms they were bitter that we limited
our toilet rooms only to the Basement and that we
had separate drinking fountain. Here is where they
slipped for I can understand their not knowing
about our toilet rooms on upper floors, but they
should know that we did not separate our drinking
fountain. This must have been a part of their
memorized instructions. Their complaint is that
children often have to go and they can not be made
travel several floors. They just can't wait.

I am having Mr. Stephenson look into the possibility
of converting a white men's toilet to colored women
and would like your thoughts on this move.

This matter was talked out with Mr. Levine and
Mr. Luft. The plan is to have you pick up the
matter from here and handle as you see it in the
best interests of the store.

An investigation has been made of the women.
Mrs. Goldberg let it be known that she lived in
Detroit at one time. Mrs. Ewing works at
Sakowitz.

The memo from the previous page is continued here. Note that the customers involved were not asking that the restaurant facilities be integrated, but rather that equal restaurants be available for African Americans.

Three women picket the Azalea Terrace, Foley's main lunchroom. Note the hastily provided "closed" signs.

In this photograph is a sit-in at the main floor lunch counter by Texas Southern University students with passersby gazing in from outside.

Here are two more scenes of the student sit-in at the main floor fountain. The blinds have now been shut.

Picketers work the sidewalk outside the Lamar Street entrance to Foley's.

Tom Stevenson, a superintendent for Foley's, talks to picketers on Main Street.

ORM 700.052

FROM: **TO:** _Lee Shiffick_

2/19/63

Dr. J. B. Whitfield (colored) came in with $300 wig his wife (cash sale) had purchased here. Said he wanted to report racial discrimination.

He said his wife was told to bring wig in for styling. When he came in today, was told we did not service colored people. (Colored people are referred to a certain beauty school and salon for styling of wigs.)

Mrs. Donnelly handled with Mr. Dewald and Mrs. Smith (Beauty Salon).

We accepted the wig; will call his wife to find out how to be styled and he will pick up here in Executive Office tomorrow.

Dated 1963, an inter-store memo to Bill Shiffick, vice president of operations, reports a customer problem concerning the styling of a wig in the beauty salon.

THE NATIONAL ASSOCIATION FOR THE ADVANCEMENT OF COLORED PEOPLE

OF HOUSTON

2206 Dowling Street - Room 211   Houston, Texas 77003   228-0141

November 11, 1969

Mr. Robert W. Dundas, Sr.
Vice President
Foley's
P. O. Box 1971
Houston, Texas 77001

Dear Mr. Dundas:

We are very pleased to inform you that the Awards Committee of the NAACP of Houston has chosen Foley's to receive "The Houston Community Service Award:"

"To be presented to an organization or business concern for exemplary performance, in promoting equal opportunity for the economically dis-advantaged, and in promoting community, social and economic improvement without regard for race creed or ethnic origin."

If Foley's will accept this award we should like to receive descrip-tion of some of the things that Foley's has done and is now doing to promote equal opportunity, from your point of view. We should also like to know the name and position of the person who will accept the award on behalf of Foley's.

Sincerely yours,

C. Anderson Davis

CAD/gec

A letter dated November 1969 states that the NAACP of Houston had chosen Foley's to receive their "Houston Community Service Award." It was given to recognize a business that through exemplary performance promoted equal opportunity regardless of race, creed, or ethnic origin. Thus, the final stamp of approval of Foley's many efforts over the years by way of integration, offering of store credit to minorities, and hiring of minorities was received.

This advertisement promoted the Men's Grill, located on the second floor in the men's clothing department that served lunch to only men.

Women picket the Men's Grill. Soon the name was changed and women had equal access to the grill.

Seven

ORGANIZATIONAL DEVELOPMENT

One thing more than any other that defined the corporate culture at Foley's, was the fact that a very high percentage of its executive organization was developed from its executive training program. Whether it was the merchandising organization, the store's organization, or the sales supporting group, the staff, with very few exceptions, had come from college, entered the training program, and began climbing the promotion ladder. There was also a great deal of interchange between the three groups. It was common practice for an assistant buyer to then move to a position in a branch store and then to return back to the merchandise pyramid. Most of the store managers and regional managers had moved back and forth between stores and merchandising. This gave each group an understanding of the way the other group worked and what problems each faced. This developed a cohesiveness that ensured the entire organization worked in the best interest of the store.

Milton Berman and Stewart Orton were a magnificent team that worked together to grow the Foley's organization. They had one principle that more than any other made Foley's successful and kept its executives from being enticed by competitors: Push decision-making to the lowest possible level and give each person the authority to go along with the responsibility of the job. Berman and Orton did not micromanage the people who reported to them and this philosophy permeated the entire organization. This factor, plus the "promote from within" philosophy combined to make Foley's successful and unique from many other stores, including many of the Federated Department Stores.

In 1951, Foley's recognized the importance that women executives would play in the future by appointing the first woman divisional merchandise manager of Feminine Accessories, Helen Orfan. Divisional merchandise managers (DMM) were middle-management executives who were responsible for a group of buyers, usually within a single merchandise category. Fourteen years later a second woman was appointed as DMM, Anita Diamond, of the Dress division. It was not until the 1970s that women became increasingly involved in middle- and upper-level management positions, although the 1960s saw many women in positions such as buyer and holding important positions in the branch organization. It is impossible to list every female executive who helped Foley's become the dominant store in Texas, but they held positions at the highest level in merchandising, sales promotion, and the store's organization.

Also of significance was the number of Foley's executives that were promoted by Federated Department Stores to head other stores in their group. Charles Luft was the first, going to Sanger-Harris in Dallas. Orrin Bradley became head of Milwaukee's Boston Store. Donald Stone went to Sanger-Harris in Dallas and from there to Federated Department Store's central office in Ohio as vice chairman. Jim Zimmerman went to Rich's Department Store and eventually became the head of Federated Department Stores. Lasker Meyer went to Abraham & Straus in Brooklyn before returning to Foley's. Matt Spiegel went to Goldsmith's in Memphis, with Roger Knox following to fill the president's post. Although other Federated Department Store divisions filled the top positions at some stores, Foley's probably supplied more than any other.

In the 1980s, some of Foley's executives moved to other stores and fields. Maxine Kelly became head of a major jewelry manufacturer in New York. Janet Gurwitch held a top merchandising position at Neiman Marcus in Dallas before leaving to start her own cosmetic company. The current head of Neiman Marcus, Karen Katz, is a former Foley's executive. Linda Wachner, who was an extremely successful intimate apparel buyer at Foley's, left to become the buyer at Macy's New York. From there she joined Warner Brothers Company, an intimate apparel manufacturer that she headed and built into a major conglomerate, Warnaco.

When Milton Berman retired in early 1979, Stewart Orton became chairman and CEO and Lasker Meyer became president. That lasted only a year because Federated Department Stores moved Meyer to Abraham & Straus in Brooklyn as chairman and CEO. John Utsey then became president of Foley's. Orton retired at the beginning of 1982 and Meyer returned to become chairman and CEO with Utsey remaining president.

If Meyer had known what awaited him he might have had second thoughts about returning to Foley's. The year 1981 was the most profitable one in Foley's history and made it one of the top contributors to Federated Department Store's profit. Shortly after his return, the OPEC energy crisis hit the United States, and Houston, the energy capital of the United States, was the first to feel its effects. Houston at that time was practically a one-industry city with headquarters of most major oil companies such as Exxon, Texaco, and Shell, as well as most of the major oil field equipment companies. Layoffs began with ensuing ripple effect on most segments of the Houston economy. Foley's, which had enjoyed incomparable growth along with the Houston economy during the previous decades, began to feel the effects of diminishing sales and profits, even before other metropolitan areas of Texas like Dallas, Fort Worth, and Austin whose economies were not so closely tied to the oil industry. That economic downturn lasted most of the 1980s.

To further complicate matters, Houston experienced at the same time a major retail expansion. Retail companies that had envied Houston's growth and Foley's success made major plans to enter the metropolitan Houston market. Dillard's bought Joske's, Macy's opened four large stores, Mervyn's opened multiple stores, as did Target (both divisions of the Dayton-Hudson Company.) Foley's had committed to a major expansion program both in Houston and other Texas cities.

During the period of the recession, Federated management, in the form of chairman and CEO Howard Goldfeder, and Donald Stone, vice chairman of Federated Department Stores to whom Foley's management reported, made frequent trips to Foley's to meet with management, review strategy, and critique problems. They were full partners with Foley's management and if they had any serious concerns about the way the company was run or suggestions about how to offset the oil recession or the new competition, they were not expressed.

Max Levine came to Foley's from the F&R Lazarus Company, another Federated Department Stores division, when Foley's was purchased in 1945. He retired in 1966.

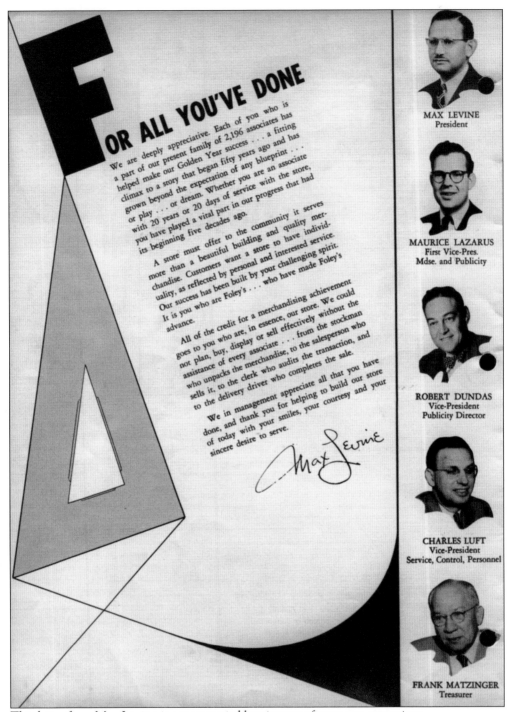

FOR ALL YOU'VE DONE

We are deeply appreciative. Each of you who is a part of our present family of 2,196 associates has helped make our Golden Year success . . . a fitting climax to a story that began fifty years ago and has grown beyond the expectation of any blueprint . . . or play . . . or dream. Whether you are an associate with 20 years or 20 days of service with the store, you have played a vital part in our progress that had its beginning five decades ago.

A store must offer to the community it serves more than a beautiful building and quality merchandise. Customers want a store to have individuality, as reflected by personal and interested service. Our success has been built by your challenging spirit. It is you who are Foley's . . . who have made Foley's advance.

All of the credit for a merchandising achievement goes to you who are, in essence, our store. We could not plan, buy, display or sell effectively without the assistance of every associate . . . from the stockman who unpacks the merchandise, to the salesperson who sells it, to the clerk who audits the transaction, and to the delivery driver who completes the sale.

We in management appreciate all that you have done, and thank you for helping to build our store of today with your smiles, your courtesy and your sincere desire to serve.

Max Levine

MAX LEVINE
President

MAURICE LAZARUS
First Vice-Pres.
Mdse. and Publicity

ROBERT DUNDAS
Vice-President
Publicity Director

CHARLES LUFT
Vice-President
Service, Control, Personnel

FRANK MATZINGER
Treasurer

This letter from Max Levine is accompanied by pictures of some top executives.

BOB MILIUS

HENRY BRAWN

EXECUTIVE LEADERS

MERCHANDISING

BOB TODD

LOUIS KEEFER

DEWITT UNTERMEYER

BILL SHIFFICK
General Supt.

M. J. TIMMONS
Controller

LESTER DEWALD
Personnel

Our Golden Year celebration officially began in the early morning, on Monday, January 30. While four score businessmen and a handful of early morning shoppers watched curiously, the mayor of Houston pulled a switch that started something the likes of which the people of the Southwest had never seen before. It was a fantasy, a breath-taking miniature of a dream of Houston in the year 2000. The Vista Window display was typical of Foley's and its 50 years of growth. Before the mayor started the "Houston, 2000 A.D." window exhibition, he and representatives of 74 businesses and industries attended Foley's Golden Year breakfast in the Azalea Terrace. These businesses, like Foley's, all had a conspicuous part in Houston's growth and prosperity in the first half of the Twentieth Century. As toastmaster at the breakfast, former Governor W. P. Hobby said: "These industries parlayed an overgrown village on a muddy bayou into the metropolis of the South and the nation's second port." With the event, Foley's Golden Year was under way. This occasion touched off an 11-month celebration of feature events in magnificent window displays and special merchandising promotions. Seven of these months have passed and we have watched these Golden Year events come to life. Here in the Anniversary month of September we pay tribute to 1950, with a review of the events which were included in the Blueprints of our Golden Year.

Pictured are the top merchandising and operations executives in 1950.

Milton Berman, chairman and CEO of Foley's, was sent to replace Max Levine in 1964. He had previously been executive vice president of Abraham & Straus in Brooklyn.

Stewart Orton, president, came to Foley's with Milton Berman as president and head of merchandising, advertising, and stores. Lasker Meyer was appointed general merchandise manager of the upstairs fashion divisions.

port ✳ foley ✳ o

VOL. 26, NO. 52   DECEMBER 31, 1971

GEORGE S. COHEN

Former Foley's Owner Stricken

George S. Cohen, businessman, philanthropist and longtime former owner of Foley's, succumbed to a heart attack at his home Dec. 22 at the age of 86.

Mr. Cohen often said that he had but two ambitions—to be a merchant and to be captain of an ocean-going vessel. The first ambition was fulfilled when he and his late father, Robert I. Cohen, Sr., purchased the store in 1917 from the brothers Foley, Jim and Pat.

Though Mr. Cohen sold Foley's in 1945 to Federated Department Stores, Inc., he kept an office on the ninth floor Downtown, devoting most of his time to Houston arts and charities.

Throughout his life, Mr. Cohen's enthusiasm for Houston and its growth was boundless. He chartered and brought to Houston its first passenger liner from Europe in 1925, and played a role in the development of the city's first airlines.

Most of all, Mr. Cohen was a friend of the people of Houston—a philanthropist, patron of the arts and friend of Rice University.

Saying, "It permitted my use of the Commandment 'Honor Thy Father and Mother,' " he gave the Cohen House, a faculty club, to Rice in 1927 in memory of his parents.

Mr. Cohen was born in Galveston and worked in his father's store there, getting his own order book at age ten. He was educated at Peekskill Military Academy New York.

Sympathy is expressed to his wife, Mrs. Esther Meyer Cohen of Houston, and other relatives of the family.

TRIO NAMED TO NEW POSTS

OLIVER, MILLER AND ROSENFELD ASSUME NEW DUTIES JAN. 10

In a trio of executive appointments effective Jan. 10, 1972, Robert Oliver has been appointed assistant store manager—merchandising at Almeda; Harris Miller has been named divisional sales manager—fashion wear and accessories and budget apparel and accessories at Sharpstown; and Enid Rosenfeld has been promoted to divisional sales manager—fashion at Northwest.

Mr. Oliver joined Foley's in August 1959 as an executive trainee in merchandising. He was promoted to department manager—budget junior dresses and sportswear in May 1961, and in April 1964 became the budget sportswear department manager.

He was appointed divisional sales manager—apparel, accessories and men's wear at Sharpstown in June 1967. Since November 1969, he has been responsible for fashion wear and accessories and budget apparel and accessories.

BOB OLIVER

Mr. Miller is currently divisional sales manager—soft lines at Northwest. He joined Foley's as an executive trainee in January 1963, and in March of that year was named sales supervisor in budget millinery.

(Continued on Page 2, Col. 1)

Twenty Year Club Celebrates . . .

The place? The Terrace. The happy occasion? The Twenty Year Club's annual Christmas breakfast, which was held the morning of Dec. 22. Quite a few retired associates took advantage of the opportunity to wish longtime friends and co-workers a happy holiday season, and do some last-minute Christmas shopping of their own!

This *port*Foley*o* article announced the death of George S. Cohen, who owned Foley's from 1917 to 1945. A second article announced the appointment of Bob Oliver as assistant manager of the Almeda-Genoa store. Oliver continued to rise in the store ranks, eventually because vice president of all of the combined Foley's and Sanger-Harris stores.

Bob Dundas, vice president in charge of public affairs, retired March 1, 1973, after a 49-year career at Foley's.

LASKER MEYER

MATTHEW SPIEGEL

JAMES NELSON

Three Major Executive Promotions Announced

The promotions of three top Foley's executives were announced yesterday by Milton S. Berman, Chairman of the Board.

Lasker Meyer has been named Vice President and General Merchandise Manager of the Fashion Divisions of Foley's upstairs store. He continues as a member of the Operating Committee. Mr. Meyer has previously been Vice President and General Merchandise Manager of Foley's Budget Store.

Matthew Spiegel has been appointed General Merchandise Manager of Foley's Budget Store and was named to the Operating Committee. He has been Manager of Foley's Sharpstown Store.

James Nelson has been appointed Manager of Foley's Sharpstown Store. Mr. Nelson has been Divisional Merchandise Manager of Foley's Junior, Lingerie, and Children's Departments.

"All the promotions, from within the Foley's organization, are in keeping with the store's policy of seeing that members of management are seasoned by experience in a number of merchandise areas," Mr. Berman said. Appointments are effective July 1.

On June 30, 1967, Milton Berman announced the appointment of Lasker Meyer as vice president and general merchandise manager of the fashion divisions of the upstairs store. Matt Spiegel replaced him as general merchandise manager of the budget store. Jim Nelson, who had been divisional merchandise manager of juniors, lingerie, and children's, was appointed manager of the Sharpstown store.

port ✽ Foley ✽ o

VOLUME 30, NUMBER 2   Foley's Store Newspaper   JANUARY 10, 1975

Major Promotions Announced by Foley's Management

Major promotions have been announced at Foley's by Milton S. Berman, chairman of the board and Stewart Orton, president, following the recent announcement that

MR. SPIEGEL

Donald J. Stone, vice president and general merchandise manager had been named chairman of the board of Sanger-Harris of Dallas.

Reporting to Lasker M. Meyer, the newly-named senior vice president, general merchandise manager of the upstairs store are four vice president-general merchandise managers, whose promotions will be effective February 2:

Matthew Spiegel, 40, has been named

MR. KAPLAN

vice president, general merchandise manager of the fashion division. Previously, Mr. Spiegel was vice president-general mer-

chandise manager of Foley's budget store. He joined Foley's in 1965 after being associated with the Boston Store, Milwaukee, another Federated division.

Mr. Spiegel has held a number of executive positions at Foley's, being named buyer of budget dresses in 1966, branch manager of Sharpstown in 1967, general merchandise manager of the budget store in 1968 and vice president in 1969.

A graduate of New York University with a BS degree, Mr. Spiegel and his wife Ellen are the parents of two sons and a daughter.

William J. Kaplan has been promoted to vice president, general merchandise manager of men's and children's wear. He

MR. McNAUGHT

has been a merchandise vice president in charge of men's and boys' wear. Mr. Kaplan, 48, came to Foley's in 1949 as a salesman and was named buyer of budget boys' wear in 1952, buyer of upstairs boys' wear in 1954, and divisional merchandise manager of men's and boys' in January 1959. He was promoted to merchandise vice president in January 1973.

A native of Massachusetts, Mr. Kaplan holds a degree from Brown University, and has attended graduate school at Harvard, Brown and Boston University. He is a member of the board of directors of the Sam Houston Area Council of Boy Scouts and is on the Advisory Council of the University of Texas at Austin, School of Business. Mr. Kaplan has three children and is married to the former Nancy Richmond.

Donald McNaught, 45, has been promoted to vice president, general mer-

chandise manager, decorative home furnishings. His responsibilities will also include home textiles and housewares. Mr. McNaught joined Foley's as a trainee in

MR. FRIEDMAN

1955, was named buyer of luggage in 1957, budget linens buyer in 1959, was promoted to buyer of men's furnishings and sportswear in 1963, and was named divisional merchandise manager of fashion home furnishings in 1966.

A native of New Jersey, Mr. McNaught is a graduate of the University of Texas and holds a degree in business administration. He and his wife Lianne are the parents of two sons.

MR. KAMINSKY

Edward Friedman, 40, has been promoted to vice president, general mer-

Continued on page 2, col. 3

On December 29, 1974, Donald Stone, previously general merchandiser of the men's and home divisions, was promoted to chairman and chief executive officer of Federated Department Store's Sanger-Harris division, headquartered in Dallas. Lasker Meyer was then promoted to the new post as senior vice president and general merchandise manager of all upstairs merchandise divisions at Foley's. Following the promotions of Stone and Meyer, five new general merchandise managers were appointed: Matt Spiegel, Feminine Fashion; Bill Kaplan, Men's and Children's; Don McNaught, Decorative Home Furnishings; Ed Friedman, Major Home Furnishings; and Harold Kaminsky, Budget Store. To replace them, seven new divisional merchandise managers were appointed.

| **DAVID HAMILTON** | **DICK WILSON** | **LOWELL WHITLOCK** | **DENNIS REAVES** |

Seven Divisional Appointments Announced

Seven promotions at the divisional level have been announced by Foley's management, which will become effective on February 1.

David Hamilton

David L. Hamilton has been promoted to divisional merchandise manager of the furniture departments and the Design Studio. He joined Foley's in 1964 as a trainee, was promoted to assistant department manager in 1965, and the following year, to group sales manager at Pasadena. In November 1966, he was promoted to buyer of bedding, and in March 1970, added contemporary furniture to his responsibilities.

A native of Enid, Oklahoma, Mr. Hamilton holds BS and MBA degrees from Oklahoma State University.

Dick Wilson

Dick Wilson has been promoted to divisional merchandise manager of fashion fabrics, patterns, art needlework, sewing machines, linens, sheets, blankets, the Bath Shop and draperies. A native Arkansan and a graduate of the University of Arkansas, Mr. Wilson joined Foley's in 1961 as a trainee. The following year, he was promoted to assistant department manager of budget lingerie, and later, of the boys' area. He was appointed group sales manager at Sharpstown in 1964, and was named buyer of men's hats and shoes in 1967. In 1970, he became buyer of linens. In April 1973 he was promoted to divisional sales manager of home furnishings at Sharpstown.

Lowell Whitlock

Lowell Whitlock's responsibility has been changed to divisional merchandise manager of the housewares departments, toys, luggage and sporting goods. Mr. Whitlock came to Foley's in September 1961 as a trainee, and shortly thereafter was named head of stock in housewares. In 1962, he was promoted to assistant department manager in the housewares area, and later that year, was appointed group sales manager at Sharpstown.

In 1965, Mr. Whitlock was named buyer of lamps, and in 1967, of sheets and blankets. In 1970 he was promoted to divisional sales manager of hardlines and men's at Northwest, and in January 1973, divisional sales manager of home furnishings at Sharpstown. In April of that year, he was promoted to divisional merchandise manager, toys, fabrics, sporting goods and luggage.

A native of Fletcher, Oklahoma, Mr. Whitlock graduated from Texas Tech University with a BBA degree.

Dennis Reaves

Dennis Reaves has been promoted to divisional merchandise manager of the children's departments and maternity. He came to Foley's in 1967 as a trainee, and was promoted to assistant department manager of toys in 1968. In January 1969, he was named a group sales manager at Sharpstown, and in August of the same year, was promoted to senior assistant department manager. Two months later, he was appointed to buyer of china and glassware and, in 1972, he went to Almeda as divisional sales manager of softlines.

A native of Loudon, Tennessee, Mr. Reaves holds a BBA degree from the University of Texas.

(Continued on page two)

DEEP-SEA FISHING JANUARY 19

Who cares if it snows... as long as the waves aren't 10 feet tall? Seriously, Foley's deep-sea fishermen will have another chance to brave the elements this Sunday, when the thrice-cancelled trip is again scheduled. Same time.... 2:00

a.m.... same place... Party Boats in Freeport. Let's hope this time we have beautiful weather!

Seven divisional manager appointments were announced following the reorganization of the merchandising organization.

LINDA HAGLER

JUDY GRAY

TINA PAPPAS

Seven Divisional Promotions, Continued.

Linda Hagler

Linda Hagler has been promoted to divisional merchandise manager of all junior departments and Point of View sportswear. Ms. Hagler joined Foley's in 1960 as a trainee. She was head of stock in budget piece goods, an assistant department manager in budget children's, and a group sales manager at Sharpstown. She was named buyer of young juniors' in 1963, and was appointed buyer of junior sportswear in 1965. In March of 1973, she was promoted to divisional merchandise manager of children's wear.

A native Texan, Ms. Hagler is a graduate of Texas Tech University with a BS degree.

Judy Gray

Judy Gray has been promoted to divisional merchandise manager of Pacesetter and Willowick sportswear, and the blouse departments. Ms. Gray began her career at Foley's in 1964 as a trainee. She was named an assistant department manager in 1965, a buyer in junior high and Girl Scouts in 1966, buyer in corsets and bras in 1969 and, later that year, she moved to Willowick sportswear.

A native of Oklahoma, Ms. Gray holds a degree from Oklahoma State University.

Tina Pappas

Tina Pappas has been named divisional manager — fashion director. A Wisconsin native, Ms. Pappas received her merchandising training in Chicago, and joined Foley's in February 1961. In August of the same year, she was named head of stock in millinery, then coats, and in February 1962, was promoted to fashion coordinator of children's. Her responsibilities later encompassed Foley's branches, Sharpstown and Pasadena. In September 1968, Ms. Pappas was promoted to fashion director.

Of the seven new divisional merchandise managers, three were women, which resulted in a total of four women managers. Shirley Gard was the divisional manager of Dresses and Coats, and Linda Hagler was divisional manager of all Junior Departments and Point of View (Misses Contemporary Sportswear.) Judy Gray was divisional manager of all Misses Sportswear Departments, and Tina Pappas was divisional manager and fashion director for the entire store.

Two other women who distinguished themselves in the fashion industry should be mentioned. Janet Gurwitch, who began in Foley's training program, rose to the ranks of divisional manager of the Juniors department. She left Foley's in 1989 and became executive vice president of Neiman Marcus in Dallas. After several years there, she left to begin her own cosmetic company, Laura Mercier. Maxine Kelly, who returned to Foley's after a distinguished career in manufacturing, became vice president and general merchandise manager of the fashion divisions.

MIMI IRWIN

Mimi Irwin Named DMM

Announcement has been made of the promotion of Mimi Irwin to divisional merchandise manager of junior departments and Point of View sportswear. The appointment was effective May 24, 1976.

Ms. Irwin joined Foley's in August 1967 as an executive trainee and was promoted to assistant department manager of children's accessories in March 1968 and later moved to junior dresses. In February 1969, she was promoted to group sales manager at the Almeda store and in May 1970, returned Downtown as senior assistant department manager of junior dresses and coats. In March of the following year, she was named department manager of those same departments. In January 1974, she was appointed department manager of Point of View and in January 1976, the Young Signature Shop was added to her responsibilities.

Ms. Irwin received her B.S. degree in clothing and textiles from the University of Texas.

Another woman in a senior management position at Foley's was Doreen Leibovitz, who was appointed to the position of vice president of personnel.

Within two years, Linda Hagler left the store to be married in another state. Mimi Irwin was promoted to replace her.

Doreen Leibovitz

Foley's management is pleased to announce the appointment of Doreen Leibovitz to the position of vice president — personnel effective February 10, 1986.

Doreen is an honors graduate of the University of Oklahoma where she received a bachelor's degree in English and Journalism. She began her career with Foley's in July 1971 as a downtown training coordinator.

By 1972, Doreen assumed the duties of corporate training consultant. In September of 1974, she was appointed merchandising, recruiting and placement manager. The following year, Doreen was promoted again, this time to manager of executive recruiting and placement. She held this position until being named group manager, executive development and training in February 1979. Later in 1979, Doreen assumed the duties of executive development director.

Myrna Phillips New Advertising Director

The appointment of Myrna Phillips as Foley's advertising director was recently announced by Lee M. Dubow, vice president in charge of sales promotion.

The new divisional manager of advertising joined Foley's September 1, replacing Roy Boutillier.

A native of New York, Ms. Phillips was advertising manager of Gimbel's of New York for two and one-half years. Prior to her assignment at Gimbel's, she was copy supervisor for hard goods at Abraham & Straus, a Federated division in Brooklyn, N.Y., for 13 years.

Ms. Phillips has one son, eight year-old Frank Douglas Greenberg.

Myrna Phillips was hired in 1968 as Foley's advertising director. Shortly after Lasker Meyer became senior vice president of the upstairs store, he promoted her to vice president of advertising.

Lennie Klingaman was a certified public secretary and executive secretary for Lasker Meyer. Klingaman was a perfectionist who went to school on her own time to become a certified public secretary in order to do her job in a most professional manner.

OFFICE OF THE PRINCIPALS

OVP
PUBLIC AFFAIRS
A.J. Gallerano

CHRMN OF THE BOARD
& CEO
Milton S. Berman

OVP
RESEARCH
James Baker

PRESIDENT
Stewart Orton

SR VP & GMM
MERCHANDISING
Lasker Meyer

VP & GMM
FASHION
Matthew Spiegel

VP & GMM
MEN'S & CHILDREN'S
William Kaplan

VP & GMM DEC
HOME FURNISHINGS
John Utsey

VP & GMM
MAJOR HOME FURN
Edward Friedman

VP & GMM
BUDGET STORE
Harold Kaminsky

VP & PUBLICITY
DIRECTOR
Myrna Phillips

DMM
INT APPL & SMLWRS
Joseph Sternberg

DIV'L MGR
FASHION DIR
Tina Pappas

DMM
MEN'S
Robert Lindley

DMM
TOYS, HSWRS, SPTG
GOODS, LUGGAGE
Lowell Whitlock

DMM
APPL, RADIO & TV
Laddie Luljak

DMM
MEN'S, BOYS',
HOME FURNISHINGS
Roger Knox

DIV'L MGR
VISUAL PRESENTATION
& SPECIAL EVENTS
Joseph Hoppe

DMM
ACCES. FINE JWLRY
& SHOES
Bud Goldstein

DMM
CHILDREN'S
& MATERNITY
Dennis Reaves

DMM
HOME TEXTILES
Richard Wilson

DMM
FURNITURE &
DESIGN STUDIO
David Hamilton

DMM
ACCESS. INT APP'L
& CHILDREN'S
Gary Gladding

DMM
WOMEN'S & MISSES
DRESSES
Shirley Gard

DMM
MEN'S CLOTHING & SHOES
William Schleisner

DMM
JUNIORS & POINT OF
VIEW SPTSWR
Mimi Irwin

BRANCH STORE MGR
PASADENA
Harris Miller

BRANCH STORE MGR
GREENSPOINT
Bob Oliver

OVP
SHARPSTOWN
Glenn Kittinger

BRANCH STORE MGR
NORTHWEST
Click Eisenberg

BRANCH STORE MGR
ALMEDA
Bud Frazier

BRANCH STORE MGR
MEMORIAL
Bob Harris

DMM
PACESETTER & WILLOWICK
SPORTSWEAR & BLOUSES
Judy Gray

foley*s

P ORGANIZATION

SR VP OPERATIONS
& CONTROL
William Shiflick

VICE PRESIDENT
FINANCE AND CONTROL
Wm. J. Plexco

VP OPERATIONS
Douglas Koy

VP
ORG DEVELOPMENT
Richard Bynum

DIV'L VICE PRESIDENT
ACCOUNTING &
FINANCIAL REPORTING
Dan Andrews

DIV'L VICE PRESIDENT
CREDIT & LOSS PREVENTION
Leroy Zochert

DIV'L MGR
OPERATION SERVICES
Arden Ristau

DIV'L MGR
CONSTRUCTION &
STORE DEVELOPMENT
Mahlon Bradford

DIV'L MGR
PERSONNEL
Vincent Rachal

DIV'L MGR
ADMINISTRATION
Jerry Stewart

DIV'L MGR
LOSS PREVENTION
Carl Donnelly

DIV'L VP
DISTRIBUTION CENTER
Earl McMullin

DIV'L MGR
FOODS
Vince Broomhall

DIV'L MGR MANPOWER
DEVELOPMENT
Richard Dunn

DIV'L MGR
DATA PROCESSING
Reginald Kennerly

DIV'L MGR
RECEIVING/MARKING
Kenneth Davis

DIV'L MGR
MERCHANDISE INFO SYSTEMS
David Carrington

DIV'L MGR DELIVERY
& PERSONNEL
Terry Bacigalupo

NOTE: The level of a position on this chart does
not indicate its level of responsibility

Date as of 7/1/78
Prepared by the office of
Corporate Training & Development

This organizational chart shows the company's leadership in 1978.

The merchandise managers are pictured at their annual Christmas lunch. The tradition included updating a scrapbook called "The Book of the Departed," so named because each year a photograph of the current group was added, along with a footnote about those who had left the store. The participants for this year's lunch were, from left to right, (first row) Lasker Meyer, Linda Hagler, Shirley Gard, Bill Kaplan, and Bob Lindley; (second row) Matt Spiegel, Lowell Whitlock, Harris Miller, Jim Ivester, Joe Sternberg, Laddie Luljak, Ed Friedman, Harold Kaminsky, Bud Goldstein, and Donald Stone.

Stewart Orton, former president of Foley's, became chairman and chief executive officer on February 3, 1979, when Milton Berman retired. Lasker Meyer, the former senior vice president of merchandising and sales promotion, became president.

port✱foley✱o
FOLEY'S STORE NEWSPAPER — VOLUME 33, NUMBER 26 ● DECEMBER 5, 1978 SPECIAL EDITION

Stewart Orton and Lasker Meyer announced as new top management team at Foley's

Stewart Orton

Lasker M. Meyer

Federated Department Stores, Inc., the parent company of Foley's, has announced that Stewart Orton, president of Foley's, will become its chairman and chief executive officer on February 3, 1979, when Milton S. Berman, who now holds the position, retires. At the same time, Lasker M. Meyer, senior vice president of merchandising and sales promotion, will succeed Mr. Orton as president.

Stewart Orton, the chairman-designate of Foley's, began his career at Shillito's in his hometown of Cincinnati, where he rose to vice president and general merchandise manager. He went on to become executive vice president of the Boston Store in Milwaukee, and put in a stint at Federated Corporate Office before being named vice president and general merchandise manager of Foley's in 1964. He was named president of Foley's in 1967.

A graduate of the University of Michigan, Mr. Orton and his wife, Hanni, have two children, John Orton, an attorney in Houston, and Mrs. Charles Loucks, also of Houston.

Mr. Orton is very active in Houston civic and cultural activities. He is presently a director of the Federal Reserve Bank of Dallas and president of St. Joseph Hospital Foundation in Houston, in addition to serving on the boards of directors of the Houston Chamber of Commerce, Better Business Bureau, United Fund, Museum of Fine Arts, Combined Arts Corporate Campaign, and the University of Houston Foundation.

Lasker Meyer, Foley's new president and a third generation Houstonian, joined Foley's in 1959

as a buyer and held a variety of positions before being named senior vice president of merchandising and sales promotion in 1975.

Mr. Meyer attended Rice University prior to serving in the Navy during World War II. He has been an active volunteer with the United Fund of Houston for a number of years and is currently chairman of the P.A.I.R. committee as well as a member of the executive committee, and the Houston Clean City Commission.

He and his wife, Beverly, have two daughters, Mrs. Marvin Brown and Mrs. Craig Sellinger.

In making the announcements, Ralph Lazarus, chairman, and Harold Krensky, president of Federated, joined in saying, "Milt Berman has been one of the truly great merchants in the Federated organization. One has only to look at the extraordinary growth of Foley's to get some conception of his great skills. From the bottom to the top, both at Foley's and Federated, Milt Berman has the enduring affection and admiration of all our associates."

Mr. Orton and Mr. Meyer concurred, saying, "Milt has guided Foley's for the past 15 years, through its most dramatic period of growth. We will try to match Milt's remarkable record by keeping Foley's growing through the 1980's and beyond. To that end, we have already announced very dramatic plans, including expansion of two existing stores and building three new ones during the next five years. Additional stores, both in and outside of Houston, are contemplated and will be announced in the months ahead."

port✱foley✱o
SPECIAL EDITION — VOLUME 35 ● NUMBER 2 JANUARY 28, 1980

Utsey new president; Meyer named A&S chairman
Spiegel, Friedman, Plexco elevated to senior vice presidents

John B. Utsey will become president of Foley's, succeeding Lasker M. Meyer, who is leaving to join Abraham & Straus in New York as chairman and chief executive officer.

Under Foley's traditional two-man top management team concept, sales-supporting divisions (branch store management, operations and finance) will report to Mr. Utsey. Reporting to Stewart Orton, chairman and chief executive officer, will be merchandising, sales promotion and personnel divisions.

In making the announcements, Mr. Orton and Harold Krensky, president of Federated Department Stores, Inc., parent company of Foley's and Abraham

& Straus, joined in praising Mr. Meyer as a "superb merchant" who has made a major contribution to Foley's "extraordinary growth."

Mr. Orton also pointed out that John Utsey's prior involvement in store operations would make for a smooth transition that augurs well for Foley's extensive expansion and building program.

In other related changes, Foley's has announced the appointment of three senior vice presidents: Matthew Spiegel, for women's, men's and children's; Edward Friedman, for home furnishings and budget store; and Jerry Plexco, for finance.

All appointments are effective February 15, 1980.

John B. Utsey

John B. Utsey

John B. Utsey joined Foley's in 1961 as an assistant department manager, and after a career as a buyer, was promoted to divisional sales manager of hards lines and men's wear at Northwest. In 1969, he was promoted to divisional merchandise manager of the budget store's men's, boys' wear and home furnishings areas. In March 1973, he was appointed manager of the Northwest store and in August 1975, was named vice president and general merchandise manager of decorative home furnishings. On February 3, 1979, he was appointed vice president of stores and in September of that year was given additional responsibilities for operations. A graduate of Baylor University with a B.B.A. degree, he earned an M.S. degree in retail management at New York University. He and his wife, Lavelle, have two children, David and Jennifer.

Lasker M. Meyer

Lasker M. Meyer

Lasker Meyer, who was named president of Foley's on February 3, 1979, is a third-generation Houstonian. He joined Foley's in 1959 as a buyer of boys' wear, was manager of the Sharpstown store, vice president in charge of branch store operations and served as vice president and general merchandise manager of the budget store and fashion division. On February 2, 1975, he was appointed senior vice president of merchandising and sales promotion.

Mr. Meyer attended Rice University prior to serving in the Navy during World War II. He has been an active volunteer with the United Way of Houston for a number of years, and has served as chairman of the P.A.I.R. committee and member of the executive committee. He has also been a member of the Houston Clean City Commission.

He and his wife, Beverly, have two daughters, Mrs. Lynne Brown and Mrs. Craig Sellinger, and one granddaughter, Allison Sellinger.

Within a year after being named president, Lasker Meyer was asked to become chairman and CEO of Abraham & Straus, Federated Department Store's Brooklyn-based division. This was the very store that Milton Berman had come from originally. When Meyer left, John Utsey became president.

Matthew Spiegel

Edward Friedman

Jerry Plexco

Further changes in management were required. Matt Spiegel became senior vice president of Fashion and Men's; Ed Friedman became senior vice president of Home; and Jerry Plexco became the chief financial officer.

Matthew Spiegel

Matthew Spiegel joined Foley's in 1965 after being associated with the Boston Store in Milwaukee, another division of Federated. He has held a number of executive posts at Foley's, being named buyer of budget dresses in 1966, branch manager of the Sharpstown store in 1967, general merchandise manager of the budget store in 1968, and vice president in 1969. He was named vice president and general merchandise manager of the fashion division in February 1975, and in February 1979, was promoted to vice president and general merchandise manager of fashion, men's and children's divisions.

He holds a B.A. degree from New York University.

port*foley*o is published by Foley's personnel division for store associates and retirees.

Editor: Lisa S. Coles

Edward Friedman

Edward Friedman joined Foley's in 1965 as buyer of floor coverings and was named divisional merchandise manager of housewares and piece goods in October 1969. In April 1973, he was named divisional merchandise manager of furniture and the Warehouse Store, and in February 1975, was promoted to vice president and general merchandise manager of major home furnishings. He was appointed vice president and general merchandise manager of home furnishings and textiles in February 1979, and added responsibilities for the budget store in January of this year.

He holds a business degree from the University of Vermont.

Jerry Plexco

Jerry Plexco joined Foley's in December 1962 as an inventory controller. In 1964, he was promoted to internal auditor and three months later was named chief accountant. By January of 1966, he had moved into the post of assistant controller and was responsible for sales audit, payroll, cash office, layaway, mail room and the ticket center. In February 1970, he was promoted to divisional manager of receipts and disbursements and in June of the same year, was appointed controller and became a member of the store's operating committee. In 1971, he was named operating vice president— controller, and in 1974, became vice president—controller. In February 1978, he was promoted to vice president—finance and control.

A 1954 graduate of the University of Houston, he holds a B.B.A. degree in accounting.

When leaving Foley's to go to Abraham & Straus, Meyer obtained a letter from Ralph Lazarus, CEO of Federated Department Stores, that when Stewart Orton retired he would have the option of returning to Foley's as chairman and CEO. Although Orton had only been CEO for three years, Meyer expected him to remain in that position for a longer period, just as Berman had. However, Donald Stone, vice chairman of Federated Department Stores, to whom Foley's reported, and Howard Goldfeder, CEO of Federated Department Stores, made the decision that Orton should retire. Not wanting to stay in Brooklyn indefinitely, Meyer had to make the decision to return to Foley's, much to Federated Department Store management's dismay. The year 1981 had been the most successful year in Foley's history. The years 1982 to 1987, the period Meyer was chairman and CEO, were notable in that the OPEC oil crisis occurred and Houston, being the energy capital of the country, felt its effects more than any other city.

Stewart Orton announces '82 retirement; Lasker Meyer named successor

CINCINNATI, July 16, 1981 — Federated Department Stores, Inc., today announced the following changes in the top management organizations of several of its department store divisions.

Stewart Orton, chairman and chief executive officer of Foley's, Federated's Houston-based division, will retire on February 1, 1982.

Lasker M. Meyer, chairman and chief executive officer of Abraham and Straus, will become chairman and chief executive officer of Foley's upon Mr. Orton's retirement.

John W. Burden III, president of Burdines, Federated's Miami-based division, will become chairman and chief executive officer of Abraham and Straus, the company's division headquartered in Brooklyn, New York, effective September 8, 1981.

Howard Socol, executive vice president of Burdines, will become president of Burdines, effective August 24, 1981.

Commenting on the moves, Federated president Howard Goldfeder and chairman Ralph Lazarus said: "Lasker Meyer has done an excellent job of further defining and continuing turnaround of Abraham and Straus. But he expressed a desire to return to Texas, where he and his wife were born and raised and where their children and other members of their family live.

"Mr. Orton's planned retirement next year, which ends a distinguished career with Federated that began with our Shillito's division in 1937, created the opening which Mr. Meyer will fill. Stewart Orton has been an outstanding asset of Federated and has made an enormous contribution to Foley's, which he first joined as vice president and general manager in 1964. He has also been an outstanding asset of his adopted hometown of Houston, where many years of civic leadership have recently been capped by his election as chairman of the Houston Chamber of Commerce.

"John B. Utsey, president of Foley's since February of 1980, will continue in that position.

"John Burden has proved himself to be a strong and innovative merchant who performed at a very high level in his four years as president of Burdines, one of our largest and currently our fastest-growing division. As a native of Rahway, New Jersey, who received his early retail experience at Bamberger's, he has strong ties to the area served by Abraham and Straus and is ideally suited to lead the division in the continuing stages of its turnaround.

"Robert Tammero, who was president of Abraham and Straus when Mr. Meyer became chairman and chief

Stewart Orton

Lasker Meyer

executive officer in 1980, has been a major factor in the progress that has been made by the division over the last several years and will continue in that position as a partner of Mr. Burden, with whom he was previously associated at Burdines.

"Mr. Socol has a broad merchandising background and has aided Mr. Burden in the development of successful merchandising strategies for Burdines. As the new president of Burdines he will assure the kind of continuity that is important in Federated and in a fast-growing division. He will become the partner of Richard W. McEwen, who remains chairman and chief executive officer of Burdines."

Stewart Orton, 65, joined Shillito's, Federated's Cincinnati-based division, in 1937 as a stock boy and was named chairman and chief executive officer of Foley's in 1978. He had been Foley's president for the eleven previous years, executive vice president and general merchandise manager from 1965 to 1967, and vice president and general manager in 1964 and 1965. Mr. Orton spent the first 20 years of his retailing career at Shillito's, advancing to vice president and general merchandise manager of the upstairs store. He then left Federated to spend three years at the J.N. Adam Company in Buffalo as president before returning to be executive vice president of Federated's Milwaukee division, the Boston Store, from 1960 to 1963 and an operating vice president at Federated's corporate office the following year. The Cincinnati native is a director of the Bank of the Southwest, Houston Industries and its subsidiary, Houston Lighting & Power Company. Mr. Orton is a trustee of the University of Houston Foundation, St. Joseph Hospital Foundation and the Museum of Fine Arts. He is chairman of the Houston Chamber of Commerce and a director of the Houston Symphony, the Better Business Bureau and Associated Credit Services of Houston. Mr. Orton is a graduate of the University of Michigan.

Lasker Meyer became chairman and chief executive officer of Abraham and Straus in February 1980, after spending more than 20 years with Foley's. While at Foley's, Mr. Meyer worked as a department and branch manager, vice president of branch operations and a general merchandise manager. In 1975 he advanced to senior vice president and in February 1979, to division president. Mr. Meyer, 55, is a native of Houston and attended Rice University. He is a former director of the Brooklyn Chamber of Commerce and the Brooklyn Academy of Music.

116

Eight

MERGER WITH
SANGER-HARRIS

In January 1981, while serving as chairman and CEO of Abraham & Straus, Lasker Meyer was approached by two executives from Touche Ross, the Abraham & Strauss auditors, and was asked to join them in a presentation at a seminar at the National Retail Merchants Association's (NRMA) annual meeting in New York City to discuss the topic of "the retail industry, in search of real profits in the '80s." It was an immediate success, and as a result Meyer was asked to be the main speaker at the luncheon held by the NRMA in January 1982. At that luncheon, Meyer pointed out that specialty stores such as Saks and Neiman Marcus successfully merchandised their stores in various cities and states with one centralized merchandising organization, and if they could do it, why couldn't Foley's, with stores in Houston, San Antonio, and Austin, also merchandise the other Federated Department Stores division, Sanger-Harris, with stores in Dallas, Fort Worth, and elsewhere.

It was not until 1987, after Texas had suffered economic downtown due to the oil recession that started in 1982, that Federated Department Stores management made the decision to merge the two divisions under the name "Foley's" and to locate the management of the division in Houston. Meyer was to be chairman and CEO, responsible for the operation and results of the combined divisions. Michael Steinberg from Sanger-Harris was to be president, responsible for merchandising and sales promotion, and John Utsey from Foley's was to be vice chairman responsible for stores, finance, and operations. The new division reported to Donald Stone, a Federated Department

Stores vice chairman who had been a longtime executive at Foley's until he was named chairman and CEO of Sanger-Harris.

The decision was made at the Federated Department Stores management level that this would not be a "takeover" of Sanger-Harris by Foley's but rather a merger of equals. This was the beginning of a serious problem because the corporate culture of the two divisions was entirely different, not to mention the temperament of the key executives at many levels. Foley's treated all stores as equals, no matter their size or location, whereas Sanger-Harris concentrated its main efforts on a few "special stores" and treated the rest as second-class citizens. Foley's did not enter a remote location in a different city unless it had a strategy to dominate retailing in that city with one or more stores, whereas Sanger-Harris often went to a city with one store and was content to be the second- or third-largest retailer in that city. Foley's provided their remote stores with advertising commensurate with the volume of the store whereas Sanger-Harris concentrated its advertising in the Dallas area. Most of Foley's executives has grown up in the Foley's organization and had a common culture, whereas many Sanger-Harris executives came from other Federated Department Stores or retail companies. Merging these two very different corporate cultures promised problems, and they did occur. It would have been much better follow the direction of Dillard's, an Arkansas-based company that was a strong Texas retailer and had taken over other retailers. When Dillard's took over another company, it immediately removed the management of the acquired company, Dillard's systems were installed in the new division, and its corporate culture prevailed. Federated Department Stores, on the other hand, insisted that the management and buying organization of Foley's and Sanger-Harris be merged together into one organization. A series of meetings were held by the top managements of Foley's and Sanger-Harris where executives in similar positions from each division were compared based on ratings given by the management of each division. Since the culture and standards of each division were different, it was like comparing apples and oranges. As a result, many key positions at Foley's went to Sanger-Harris executives and the Foley's executive was either demoted to a lesser position or left the company. A key saying among Foley's executives after the merger was, "We kept the name, but they won the game." The end result was a division with conflicting culture and standards.

The conflict existed at many levels, but particularly between Meyer and Steinberg, each trying to operate as they had in the past, with little attempt to compromise. Federated Department Stores management had obviously not seen this potential for conflict, for it made no effort to

This was the prototype for the newest Sanger-Harris store.

anticipate it, or once it existed, to sit down with the various management executives and solve the problem. This went back to one of Federated Department Stores' strengths and, at the same time, weaknesses: the reluctance to directly interfere in the operation of its individual divisions, even if that meant a missed opportunity to strengthen the corporation as a whole.

The litany of problems that resulted from the decision to "merge" rather than "takeover" is too lengthy to cover in this book. This conflict was particularly severe in the merchandising, sales promotion, and store pyramids. When the decision to merge the two divisions had been made, Howard Goldfeder, then chairman of Federated Department Stores called Meyer, Utsey, and Steinberg into his office individually and asked for a verbal commitment from each that they would stay with the merged division for at least three years. In spite of that, in November 1987, Stone came to Foley's and met with Meyer in his office, at which time he asked Meyer to take early retirement, effective immediately. Each executive, no matter the level, received an annual review from the person he reported to. Meyer's last three reviews had all been outstanding. Stone gave no reason for his request and, when questioned, got up and left the office.

Meyer, with 29 years of corporate experience, knew that Stone could not have made that decision without corporate approval. He went to see Stewart Orton, now retired, for whom he had worked for 16 years. Orton advised him not to fight the decision in order to not increase conflict in the new division. Meyer accepted his advice—a decision he ultimately regretted.

Levy's, Sanger Harris and Foley's
A new chapter unfolds in retail history

With a combined history of over 300 years of successful retailing, the new Foley's is a melting pot full of great ideas, resources and personnel. Our bright future would not be possible however, if not for the strong foundation laid by our retailing forefathers.

The first side of our historical triangle begins with Levy's. In 1903, Mr. and Mrs. Jacob Levy travelled a dusty wagon trail to Douglas, Arizona, where they founded the Red Star store. After years of success, the Levy's decided to expand their fortunes into Tucson, where in 1931, they bought Myers and Bloom, a small men's store.

Levy's became a division of Federated Department Stores in 1960, the same year the Levy's El Con Store opened. Thriving business prompted construction and by 1975, a 76,000 square foot warehouse and a three story El ̲on store were serving the Tuc- son community.

Foothills, Levy's first branch store, opened in August of 1982. This 100,000 square foot store is nestled in The Foothills Shopping Center on Tucson's Northwest side. Later that same year, the two Levy's stores joined the Dallas- based Sanger Harris division. Levy's was renamed Sanger Harris in 1985.

The history of Sanger Harris dates back to 1857 when Isaac Sanger, a jewish German immi- grant, moved from New York City to establish the first Sanger's store in McKinney, Texas. The dry goods store was so successful in serving the local trappers and ranchers, that in 1859, Isaac and his brother Lehman opened two more stores in Weatherford and Decatur. At two year intervals, three other Sanger brothers, Philip, Samuel and later Alex, joined their broth- ers in Texas.

The Sanger Brothers closed ɔp temporarily with the advent of the Civil War, but reopened their doors with the aid of the Houston and Texas Central rail- road. Using the railroad as a guide, the Sanger brothers opened ten stores between 1865

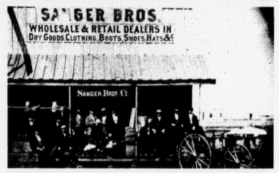

The Sanger Brothers are well known for bringing many "firsts" to retail- ing, including gas and electric lights, the use of fashion sketches, ready-to-wear clothing and escalators.

and 1873. With this expansion, Isaac moved back to New York City in 1868 to establish a perma- nent buying office. Expansion continued as Sanger's opened its headquarter store in Dallas.

Sanger's joined Federated Department Stores in 1951. Ten years later, they acquired A. Harris, another Dallas department store. This profitable combination moved to another downtown location and took on a new name, Sanger Harris. In 1965, a totally new Sanger Harris department store was opened downtown which replaced its predecessors.

Further expansion opened four stores in 1970 and three addi- tional branches were added by 1980. Sanger Harris opened its first store outside of the Dallas/ Fort Worth area in Tyler in 1981. Woodland Hills was opened in Tulsa, Oklahoma, in 1982, becom- ing the first Sanger Harris store outside Texas. Later in 1982, the two Levy's stores were added. Another Tulsa store opening occurred in 1984, as well as the first New Mexico store opening in Albuquerque. The most recent additions have been two Okla- homa City branches, opening in 1986.

While Sanger's was succeeding in the North Texas area at the turn of the century, two more promi- nent retailers were staking a claim in Southeast Texas. Pat and James Foley opened their dry goods store on Houston's Main street on Lincoln's birthday, February 12, 1900.

The Foley Brother's store grew with the blossoming metropolis. A larger location on Main street was acquired in 1908 and was then ex- panded in 1911. By the end of 1922, Foley's had become Hous- ton's largest department store.

In 1945, Foley's joined Federated Department Stores. Plans were then made to break ground for yet another location for the down- town store. In 1947 the new down- town store opened at the corner of Travis and Lamar Streets.

Houston's dynamic growth set the pace for Foley's expansion. In 1961, the first branch store opened at the Sharpstown Center. A second store followed a year later with the opening of the Pasadena branch. Five more Houston branches opened during the following ten year period.

Foley's first regional branch store opened in Austin in 1979. North Star in San Antonio was the second regional branch store, opening in 1981. By 1986, three more Houston branches were opened for business. Foley's most recent opening took place in Corpus Christi on March 2nd of this year.

With 38 locations in 11 markets, the new Foley's is a retail success story unparalleled. The sound foundation laid by the Levy's, Sanger Harris and Foley's organi- zations is a broad and well- balanced one. As a new company, we're sure to benefit from the experience and success of these three divisions. ▼

"A New Chapter Unfolds in Retail History" was the headline of this article from a Dallas newspaper tracing the history of Levy's, Sanger-Harris, and Foley's.

Nine

THE FINAL YEARS

Although 1987 was a controversial year for Foley's, in 1988 it was Federated Department Store's turn. Within months of Lasker Meyer's "early retirement," Donald Stone retired from Federated Department Store's corporate office. The company had made one major strategic mistake, in that it had too much cash in its reserve fund. It was a period of many corporate "takeovers," and it was vulnerable. The Campeau Corporation of Canada, primarily a real estate holding company, had already bought the Allied Stores in the United States. It saw Federated Department Stores as another profitable company with high cash reserves—an opportunity to increase holdings in the United States. Federated Department Stores was caught in a vise. On one hand, it was not in the best interest of the company to sell to an investor with no retail experience. On the other hand, it had a responsibility to its stockholders to accept an offer that gave the stockholders great profit. The Campeau Corporation paid much more for the company than it could possibly earn back. In order to reduce its debt, Campeau Corporation sold Foley's, its largest division, and Filene's of Boston to the May Company, another large retail group. It was not long before Federated Department Stores declared bankruptcy.

Once again, Foley's faced a culture shock. Whereas Federated Department Stores gave major decision-making—perhaps too much—to its individual divisions, May Company was clearly a company that ran according to the dictates of the corporate office. Merchandise assortments were changed and customer service suffered. Participation in community affairs, which had long been a hallmark of Federated Department Stores and Foley's, disappeared.

Within a few short years, Federated Department Stores reorganized out of bankruptcy. A new, leaner company bought the May Company, and Foley's was back in the Federated Department Stores fold—but under a local management that had not grown up in Foley's.

When Federated Department Stores was organized from a small group of individual stores, Fred Lazarus, who was elected the head of the new company, issued a document under which the new company would operate. Titled "Local Stores for Local People," it stated, "The first decision made by its founders was that Federated must never be a chain of identical stores with a common name, common wares and a common appeal to a mythical common customer. Each of the men who founded the corporations was an individual proud of the unique character of his store and proud of its reputation in his community. Each was a wise merchant, who knew that a department store must be an institution with a local personality that inspires civic and customer loyalty. So, to a Bostonian, Filene's is still as native as a Cabot. No more than one customer out of a thousand is likely to know that any of the Federated stores is part of a national group. That customer is probably a stockholder." Even before it was bought by Federated Department Stores, this was the philosophy that guided Foley's growth for nearly three-quarters of a century.

Shortly after buying the May Company, Federated Department Stores bought another large competitor, Macy's. By that time, Macy's had closed three of its four Houston stores, leaving only one in the Galleria. Whether it was swayed by Macy's reputation as the largest store in New York City, or by the national publicity given annually to Macy's Thanksgiving Day Parade and Fourth of July fireworks extravaganza in Manhattan, or whether it was the vision of a national chain under one name, Federated Department Store's management made the decision to change the corporate name and the name of the stores it owned to either "Macy's" or "Bloomingdale's." It further incorporated the individual merchandising organization into regions and Foley's became part of Macy's South, located and merchandised from Atlanta. Fred Lazarus's vision was no more.

The name change was big news in Houston. The front page of the *Houston Chronicle* business section was headlined "Storied Name Bows Out." It went on to state, "On many levels, Houston grew up, and marked its progress, with the retailer." Customers wrote letters to the paper and on the Internet telling of their early experiences at Foley's and how much the store had meant to them. Whether the new, more impersonal, Macy's engenders such loyalty remains to be seen.

As a complement to the sales floor of the early 1900s, contemporary Foley's shoppers were still able to find the latest clothing trends that were attractively displayed to catch the eye. (Photograph by Susan Meyer Sellinger.)

Depending on the store, Foley's shoppers might descend the escalator to see an expansive view of the men's department. (Photograph by Susan Meyer Sellinger.)

Over the years, the men's fragrance and grooming department grew to reflect societal changes. (Photograph by Susan Meyer Sellinger.)

The home furnishings and linens departments suggested décor for the bedroom and how to accessorize your bed. (Photograph by Susan Meyer Sellinger.)

Here is one last look at the Foley's sales floor. (Photograph by Susan Meyer Sellinger.)

COMPANY HISTORY

The company was founded in Houston, Texas, in 1900 as Foley Brothers. It was originally acquired by Federated Department Stores, Inc., in 1945.

In the 1970s, Foley's opened stores in Austin and in the 1980s opened in San Antonio. By 1987, Foley's absorbed Federated's Dallas-based Sanger-Harris chain with stores in the Dallas/Fort Worth Metroplex; Oklahoma City, Oklahoma; Tulsa, Oklahoma; Tucson, Arizona; and Albuquerque, New Mexico.

In 1988, Federated was purchased by real estate developer Campeau Corporation, which immediately sold Foley's along with Filene's to May Department Stores to finance its deal. This was fortunate, because in two short years Federated filed for bankruptcy, disassociated itself from Campeau, and merged with Campeau's other retail holding company Allied Stores. After its acquisition by May Company, Foley's closed several stores in Dallas it considered underperforming (including the downtown Dallas flagship store) and its Albuquerque, New Mexico, location, while also taking over two Lord & Taylor stores, one under construction in Oklahoma City and the other at San Antonio's Rivercenter.

Over the next decade, May spent heavily to build new stores, replace outdated stores, and refurbish existing stores. In 1993, May Department Stores consolidated May D&F into Foley's, which brought Foley's name to the Denver-Aurora, Colorado Springs, Boulder and Fort Collins-Loveland markets and reintroduced Foley's to the Albuquerque market. In 1995, the Tucson locations were transferred to May's Robinsons-May division. In 2001, Foley's expanded into Louisiana after May Co. acquired several Maison Blanche locations that had become Parisian stores from Proffitt's (now Saks Incorporated).

Foley's was reacquired by Federated when it took over May Department Stores on August 30, 2005. In 2006, Federated started the conversion of Foley's into Macy's. Soon, advertisements started to read, "Foley's—Now part of the Macy's Family." On September 9, 2006, the Foley's stores were renamed Macy's as part of Federated's nationwide rebranding of all former May locations.

TIMELINE

1900: Foley Brothers was opened by brothers Pat and James Foley, two young and enterprising Irishmen, on February 12 with $2,000 borrowed from an uncle. The 1,400-square-foot store located at 507 Main Street in Houston, Texas, was stocked with calico, linen, lace, pins, needles, and men's furnishings.

1905: With business booming, Pat and James purchased the building next door and added ready-to-wear clothing for women and children as well as millinery.

1911: The store moved to the 400 block of Main Street and was incorporated with capital of $150,000.

1916: Foley Brothers ranked third in retail volume in Houston with $400,000 in sales. The original 10 employees had grown to 150, and the company had 750 active charge accounts and 23,000 square feet of space.

1917: Pat and James sold Foley Brothers to George S. Cohen and George's father, Robert, a Galveston merchant. Foley Bros. grew tremendously under this new management and, by 1919, sales neared $1,000,000.

1922: Foley Bros. moved into a three-story building next door to 400 Main Street. Later that year, the store became the city's largest department store. Shoes, a beauty shop, and radio sets were included.

1941: When the United States entered World War II, Foley Bros. diverted the efforts of the advertising and personnel departments to bond drives and other wartime services. All sales promotions were suspended during this time.

1945: Federated Department Stores president Fred Lazarus Jr. came to Houston to visit his son, who was stationed at a nearby Army camp. He was impressed with Houston's potential.

1947: Now part of Federated, Foley's opened its doors at 1110 Main Street on October 20 in downtown Houston. Federated spent $13 million to build this new store, which was heralded by the press as the nation's "most modern department store."

1951: The first official Foley's Thanksgiving Day Parade was held.

1960–1967: Sharpstown, Foley's first branch store opened. Pasadena, Almeda-Genoa, and Northwest stores soon followed.

1974–1979: Memorial City and Greenspoint opened in Houston, and Highland Mall opened in Austin.

1980–1987: San Jacinto, North Star, Willowbrook, Barton Creek, West Oaks, Ingram Park, Deerbrook, Post Oak, and Corpus Christi opened.

1988: The May Department Stores Company acquired Foley's in Houston and Filene's in Boston from Federated.

1993: The May D&F division in Colorado and New Mexico was consolidated with Foley's, creating a 49-store division that was the largest in May Company.

1995–1998: Temple, Northwest Austin, Sugar Land, Northwest Albuquerque, Laredo, and Park Meadows opened. Fort Collins reopened after extensive remodeling. Purchased Jones & Jones in McAllen, Texas, and converted to Foley's.

2000–2004: NorthPark, Broomfield, Hurst, Baybrook Mall, Beaumont, Cielo Vista, Houston Galleria, Lake Charles, Denton, and Sunland opened. Foley's acquired one McRae's store and two Parisian stores in Louisiana. Cortana and the Mall of Louisiana in Baton Rouge and Acadiana in Lafayette joined Foley's. Memorial City and Baybrook reopened in new buildings.

2004: The May Department Stores Company acquired Marshall Field's, which was headquartered in Chicago, Illinois. May's seven divisions now included Foley's, Filene's, Robinsons-May, Famous-Barr, Hecht's, Lord & Taylor, and Marshall Field's.

2005: La Cantera, Garland, and Loveland opened. May and Federated Department Stores, Inc., announced plans to merge. The transaction closed in the third quarter.

2006: On February 1, 2006, the Foley's organization in Houston was dissolved and operation of its locations in Louisiana, Oklahoma, and Texas (except El Paso) were assumed by Atlanta-based Macy's South while operation of locations in Arizona, Colorado, New Mexico, and El Paso, Texas were assumed by San Francisco–based Macy's West. On September 9, 2006, the Foley's nameplate was replaced as part of Macy's nationwide rebranding of all former Federated locations.

www.arcadiapublishing.com

Discover books about the town where you grew up, the cities where your friends and families live, the town where your parents met, or even that retirement spot you've been dreaming about. Our Web site provides history lovers with exclusive deals, advanced notification about new titles, e-mail alerts of author events, and much more.

MADE IN THE USA

Arcadia Publishing, the leading local history publisher in the United States, is committed to making history accessible and meaningful through publishing books that celebrate and preserve the heritage of America's people and places. Consistent with our mission to preserve history on a local level, this book was printed in South Carolina on American-made paper and manufactured entirely in the United States.

This book carries the accredited Forest Stewardship Council (FSC) label and is printed on 100 percent FSC-certified paper. Products carrying the FSC label are independently certified to assure consumers that they come from forests that are managed to meet the social, economic, and ecological needs of present and future generations.

FSC
Mixed Sources
Product group from well-managed forests and other controlled sources

Cert no. SW-COC-001530
www.fsc.org
© 1996 Forest Stewardship Council

Find Your Place in History.